To Andrew

Happy Christmas & Good Luck in 1985!

Love Sheila

The Curling Companion

Books by the same author

The
Curling.
Companion

by
W. H. Murray

Richard Drew Publishing
Glasgow

First published 1981 by
Richard Drew Publishing Ltd
20 Park Circus, Glasgow G3 6BE
Scotland

ISBN 0 904002 80 2

Designed by James W. Murray
Set in Century Old Style by
John Swain & Son Glasgow Ltd
Printed and bound in Great Britain by
Butler and Tanner Ltd
Frome, Somerset

Contents

Acknowledgments

In writing this book, I have been helped first and foremost by Bob Cowan of Glasgow. He allowed me access both to his comprehensive library of curling books and to his wealth of knowledge of the game, ancient and modern. He guided me through the most recent records of curling throughout the world, gave advice on how best to use the data, and (from his wide experience of competitive play) how to interpret difficult points. He finally gave me the most valued service that an author may have – detailed criticism of the written word. If I should anywhere have fallen into error, ascribe it to me, not to him or any other of the experts consulted, whose counsel I did not invariably follow. The Publisher and I are further indebted to Bob Cowan for researching and providing photographs.

My thanks are due to Mr James Wyllie of Andrew Kay and Company, who allowed me to watch his masons make curling stones at Mauchline, explained the process, and allowed photographs to be taken; to the staff of the National Library of Scotland, the Mitchell Library of Glasgow, the British Library in London, and the Argyll & Bute District Library, who helped me to trace and find the original sources of centuries-old material, and gave access to rare books; to the Royal Caledonian Curling Club for permission to quote their Rules and to photograph stones, paintings and engravings from books in their library; to the Smith Institute, Stirling, and to the Central Scottish Ice Rink, Perth, for permission to photograph early stones; to Mr Cooper Hay for allowing us to reproduce his lithograph of Ailsa Craig; and to authors over the last five centuries, whose earlier work made my own possible.

My acknowledgments and thanks for permission to reproduce photographs go to Air Canada for those by Michael Burns of the Silver Broom world championships; Sir John Clerk for the first Grand Match; the Glasgow Herald for the Grand Match 1979; Kirkcaldy Museum for curling on Raith Lake; William Patrick Memorial Library, Kirkintilloch for curling on Lenzie Loch; Doug Maxwell for the photograph of Paul Gowsell taken by Michael Burns; the Mitchell Library for the detail from Bruegel's *Hunters in the Snow*; the Trustees of the National Galleries of Scotland for the plate of Sir George Harvey's *The Curlers*; the National Library of Scotland for John Cairnie's advertisement in the North British Advertiser; North American Curling News for curling in Wisconsin; Royal Bank of Scotland for the photograph by Cowper and Co. of Ingvill Gitmark and of the world championships, 1981; E. A. Sautter for those of *eisschiessen* and that of curling in Switzerland; Strathclyde Regional Archives for panoramic views of Switzerland in the 1920s and the photograph of curling on Stanely Loch; Uniroyal for that of Andrew McQuistin; the Librarian, University of Glasgow for the extract from *The Muses Threnodie*. All the photographs of curling stones and of their manufacture are by John Elder.

W H Murray
Loch Goil
August 1981

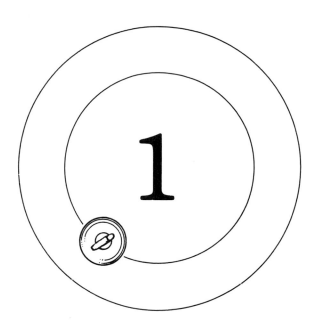

The Game and Beginnings

All day long a crowd of spectators had been gathering round Castle Loch, men, women, and children growing in numbers through the afternoon. Their breath smoked in the sharp air. The first spiel of the winter was under way. Nearly a month ago, snow had fallen as thick as a quilt over the hills and dales of Dumfries. Around the village of Lochmaben and its outlying farms, all the noise of life had been stilled, footfall muffled, the very bark of the farm dogs muted and shorn of alarm. For a day or two the world appeared as if sunk into stupor. Then a wind had come to clear the sky and to sweep the moorland snow into drifts – and now a black frost. The world again seemed spellbound, but this time with a new kind of stillness: sounds even from long distance came sharp to the ear, and footfalls rang hollow on the roadway.

Castle Loch was the largest of the five lochs that ringed Lochmaben, and over the last week hopeful curlers had been hastening there daily to test the ice for thickness. This was no white ice, which can crack like the report of a gun when it covers a big sheet of water (harmlessly if a couple of inches thick), or bends or cracks softly (time to take flight), but the black ice of sudden severe frost, viscous and durable. At an inch and a half it took skaters. For curlers more depth was wanted. The men waited in trepidation. The suspense grew nearly unbearable. Yet day by day the cold intensified. At long last the rinks could be swept out clear and keen, nearly fifty yards long, and the 'tee-ringer' fetched out to inscribe a big circle near each end named the 'house', each around a bull's eye called the 'tee'. The fear of tempting providence no longer present, the old curling stones and brooms had been carried to the rinks and challenges sent to neighbouring teams for a bonspiel.

Today the curlers had been out since early morning, getting the feel of the ice, testing its keenness, discovering any slight flaws of

'. . . the curlers had been out since early morning . . .' They still are today when, as in February 1979, the call for the Grand Match goes out.

the surface, while playing in hand and eye. They could revel in the cold. An electric energy seemed to flow through them from the crackling air, for there was no wind to shiver the body or bind the mind. On first turning out of doors their eyes had ranged in delight over gay colours, from blue sky to the tawny yellow below Queensberry Hill, where the moorland glowed through a thin lacery of windswept snow, and from sparkling crust that crunched underfoot to the black glint of swept rinks. When a stirring game is ahead, life seems more than worthwhile.

The game as always had opened quietly enough, while each team

found its form for the day and probed its opponents' strength and weakness. To each team, called a 'rink', there were four players, headed by a 'skip' or captain, and each player had two heavy round stones with a handle on top. The player's object was to slide his stone from one end of the long rink to the other, and to lay it as close to the tee as possible, or else to lay it short to guard a team-mate's stone already well placed, or to strike off an opponent's. The team with the most shots placed within the house, and most close to the tee, won the 'end' – for all sixteen stones were played from each end of the rink in turn. A game was an agreed number of ends, or else of shots scored.

Simple as the basic object was, the numerous skills of play and subtleties of tactics enthralled players and spectators alike. There was skill too in wielding the brooms. If a stone on delivery was seen to be doubtful of reaching its mark, the rest of the team pounced with their brooms, giving a rapid *brush brush brush* in front of the running stone to clear any spiculae, powder, snowflakes, leaf or whatever, and to repolish the ice. When to sweep, when to leave off, needed a skip's experience, and his team sprang to action when he cried 'Soop her up! Soop her up!' No man could stand idle. Still more was the skip needed to assess the position on the house, and decide whether his next player should 'draw' his stone (play gently for a certain spot), or try for 'a chap and lie' (strike out an opponent's stone and lie in its place), or 'raise' (promote) a stone towards the tee by bump from in front, or to lay a 'guard' stone. There were several other ways of laying a stone. The crudest was to 'red the rink' by hurling down a thunderer that cleared opponents' stones; the most skilful, to impart on delivery just the right force and twist to the handle to cause the stone at the end of its rotating slide to curl round a guard and lie by the tee, or else knock off an opposing winner. As the course of the game drew out the skills, and the scores to each side mounted neck and neck, the excitement grew intense. Every man was concentrated, every person involved.

12

Time and cold passed unheeded. Each player delivered his stone, eyes intently fixed on his mark, both on his short back-swing and after 'soling' it on the ice, for his heart and mind were still in the stone, body and hand twisting as he wanted the stone to go, crying 'Hurry, hurry, hurry!' if he thought it slow, speechless with dismay if too fast or off course. And the skip would be crying 'Soop her up!' or 'Up up!' (brooms off) as the need was. The crowd held a pin-drop silence on the slide, the only sound to break it being the long-drawn growl of the stone, a low-toned roar that has given curling its centuries-old nickname, 'the roaring game', until the stone had won or lost its mark and the crowd could vent pent-up feeling in a deep murmur or a yell of joy.

When the game began to draw to its climax, the skips between ends cast anxious glances at the sun, which was dipping to the Nithsdale hills. Its rays glittered low across the moorland snows, and nearer streamed across frozen wind-ripples leaving blue shadows along the drifts. Eastward, dusk was closing in. There under the Eskdale hills the breath of frost had been lying all day as a belt of translucent haze, dusty gold in the morning, in the early afternoon like mother-of-pearl, but with the setting sun grape-blue and opaque. There was half an hour of good daylight left for play.

The spectators were now made aware of the cold. With nipped ears and much stamping of feet, they stayed for the last two ends. Like the players themselves, and curlers of any other parish of Scotland, they came from every level of local society, landowners and labourers, farmers and shepherds, doctors and cobblers, ministers and weavers – they were on the rinks all as one in self-forgetful enthusiasm, shared tension, and common joy in good curling. Every difference they had could be sunk in the game, and every barrier

broken in plain speech. So the cold still went unheeded till the last shot was laid, the winners cheered, and the dusk had deepened in shivering starts into darkness. Then only did they stream off to pub and house for hot drinks and toddy, or neat spirits, while they lived the day's play all over again, until hunger drove them to the table. But a few enthusiasts were not finished yet. They were back again to the rink with torch and lantern, even candles if no wind were blowing up or down Annandale. The stones were kept growling down the rink until the moon rose from behind the Cheviots, and the players' shadows were cast long and thin across the ice. Before them, the high moors swelled up north in silvery waves to Queensberry Hill. The game could now go on till the early hours of morning, and be abandoned even then only with reluctance.

This scene, or something like it, allowing for differences in topography, weather, and rules, could have been true for any part of Scotland last century, and for long before if allowance were made for change in the rinks and stones. The rinks have varied in length and markings over the years. The present simple form is this:
The rink is 46 yards long. There is no set width, which is usually from 16 to 20 feet. The tees are 38 yards apart. From the tees, central lines are drawn back 4 yards, at which points foot-lines are drawn at right-angles (until recent years, the lines were called scores, but after the game had moved indoors, lines could be taped or painted under the ice). From these foot-lines the stones are delivered, and the position for the foot is marked with a hack, or roughened hollow, with its inside edge 3 inches to the side of the central line. The tee is ringed with concentric circles at radii of 4 feet and 6 feet, the last defining the house. (Other circles may be drawn.) Three other lines are drawn across the rink at right-angles to the centre line: behind each tee and 6 feet from its centre, a back line; through each tee and its outer circle, a sweeping line, or tee line; and 7 yards from each tee, the hog line. Stones are removed from the rink if they fail to pass the hog line, or pass over the back line, or touch the side lines, which are usually marked with swept snow if outdoors.

The essential implements for play have through all the centuries been only two – the stone and the broom – to which may be added one of the various kinds of metal plate needed to give the player a firm stance for delivery, especially when the ice is hardly thick enough to allow a hack to be cut.

14

Much sweeping is needed to polish the ice and clear it of powder or any other obstruction. To let the stone run free and the curler show his skill, the broom or brush is an essential tool. Every curler must carry one. Good sweeping is an essential part of the curler's art. When not to sweep, and how best to sweep, needs a keen eye and quick judgment. Games can be won or lost on it. Brooms or besoms were formerly made of broom or osier twigs, which had almost ideal flexibility. The Scots now use the straight-headed brush, closely packed with short-bristled hog's- or horse-hair. Canadians prefer their own corn broom. Sweeping is under the skip's control and subject to strict rules. The player's party may sweep from tee to tee, and only skips may sweep behind the tee. In former times, when play was outside, curlers swept from the farthest hog-score, or from tee to tee only if snow was falling or drifting.

The stones have changed much in size and shape through the years, and in weight from only a few pounds to more than a hundred, and back again to the present forty. They are now perfectly rounded, and somewhat in the shape of a Dutch cheese, highly polished, and of maximum weight 44 lb. The rocks from which they are cut and shaped have traditionally been 'whinstone' and 'granite'. Whinstone is a popular name for any hard rock that will not, like sandstone or slate, readily split when struck. Granite too was a somewhat loose term. In practice, the granite found to be most satisfactory came from Ailsa Craig until the 1950s, when quarrying began to fail. All curling stone granite comes now from Trevor in Wales. The flattened upper and under sides of the stones are given a concave or cup shape, so that they run on broad rims. The handle can be fitted to either side. Stones of this sophisticated make are relatively new in the story of curling – circular stones became the rule only after 1800. The most primitive curling stones were shaped by the natural elements alone, like the ice itself, and almost the same could be said of the broom. Man used casually three things that nature gave (the first two in abundance), and turned them into a game. The credit for this invention goes to the Scots. But when did it start? And how is that known? And why and wherefore the spread all through Scotland and beyond to nineteen other countries?

Ailsa Craig, by Clarkson Stanfield, 1854

The men who first threw stones across ice for fun were certainly not the Scots. Wherever there was ice, prehistoric men would play on it. But a point is reached – the sixteenth century – when the first signs of organized games emerge from the records. Both the written evidence and the 'hard' (the stones themselves) are found in Scotland alone. Other evidence appears from the Netherlands at that same time in the paintings of Pieter Bruegel and Jacob Grimmer.

The Scots have given several games to the world: the earliest shinty, which they had played from at least the second century AD, and so brought it with them to Dalriada (Argyll); then golf, which by 1457 had become so popular that the Privy Council damned it as checking the more needful practice of archery. In March that year they 'decreted and ordained that the futeball and golf be utterly cryit doun and nocht usit' – including football because it led to riot, which shows how little men and times change; and finally curling, of which the first report comes in the next century. These then are Scotland's three national games, in the sense of being native to the Scots.

In no other country of the world has the hard evidence of curling with stones on ice been found before its appearance in Scotland. The social historians of the sixteenth century make no mention. The earliest report of all is from Paisley Abbey in February 1541. This has recently been found at the Scottish Record Office among the papers of a Paisley notary, John McQuhin. His protocol book records in Latin a challenge to a tournament on ice made by a monk, John Slater, to the Abbot's deputy, Gavin Hamilton. Slater went on to the ice between Horgart on the west and the former Abbot's room on the east, 'and there thrice threw a stone over the ice, asserting that he was ready to carry out what had been promised on the first day of [Hamilton's] arrival, concerning the contest of throwing this kind of stone on ice.' Gavin Hamilton replied to Slater 'that he would go to the ice at the appointed place and there would contest with stones thrown on the ice.' (Where Horgart stood is now Orchard Street and the stretch of water between there and the Abbey is White Cart Water.)

The Latin text is: '*venerabilis vir dominus Joannes sclater monachus pasletensis accessit ad glaciem que est inter horgart ex occidentali et cubiculum quondam venerabilis in christo patris georgii abbatis pasletensis . . . ex orientali partibus et Ibidem ter Iecit cotem super glaciem asserens se esse paratum implere quicquid promissum erat in primo eius die adventus de certamine mittendorum super glaciem hujusmodi cotium . . . . magister gawinus hammiltoun intimavit domino Joanni sclater vt Iet ad glaciem constituti loci et Ibidem certarent cotibus super glaciem missis vt promissum erat asserens se pro parte sua respondere paratum . . . .*'

Such a formal, legal recording of a curling challenge is probably unique. It suggests the settlement of some dispute by a reversion to 'trial by combat' (introduced by William the Conqueror). If so, curling was certainly more appropriate to a monastery than the sword. A most interesting point is that the normal Latin word for stone is *lapis*. The writer seems deliberately to have chosen the word *cos* (genitive case *cotis*), which specifically means a hard rock (like the whinstone used for curling). The record was discovered in 1976 by Dr John Durkan of the Department of Scottish History at Glasgow University, when he was researching the sixteenth century history of the abbey. It was drawn to the attention of curlers in

The game of *eisschiessen* being played as it is today in Davos,
Switzerland, with Swedish participants. Behind is curling.

the following year by Sheriff David B. Smith of Kilmarnock, who is
today's foremost curling historian.

Other ice games, with one or two points of likeness to curling,
were at this same time played in Europe. Are the origins of Scottish
curling to be found in them? In Bavaria and Austria, a game many
centuries old is *eisschiessen,* or ice-shooting, played with an *eisstock*, or ice-stick. The 'stick' is a wooden, conic disc of 8 to 25
pounds' weight, 10 to 13 inches in diameter, with an iron hoop at the
lower edge. It has a handle projecting 8 or 12 inches vertically from
the middle top, and curved or tilted in the upper half. The rink is
around 33 to 60 yards long, the hacks are 20 to 60 yards apart, and
the mark is a movable oak jack, or *daube*, just 4 inches high. The
jack when knocked far out of position is still played to, the object
being to get one's own stick between the opponent's and the jack.

18

Delivering the *eisstock*

The game is for six or eight players, but the number is variable. They carry no brooms. The stick is delivered with a swing like a curler's and soled as smoothly as possible. The first record of the ice-stick game comes in two paintings by Pieter Bruegel in 1565. They are not of stone-curling as often reported.

Bruegel in his early twenties travelled from Holland to Italy in 1551. During the next four years he wandered far in the Alps, visiting Austria and the Tyrol around 1554. His biographer of 1604, Van Manders, writes, 'When he travelled through the Alps, he swallowed all the mountains and rocks, and spat them out again, after his return, on to his canvases and panels, so closely was he able to follow nature here.' Among the scenes he painted were *Hunters in the Snow* (which now hangs in the Museum at Vienna), and *Winter Landscape* (in the Brussels Delporte Collection).

Detail from Bruegel's *Hunters in the Snow*

His *Hunters* has a background of Alpine rock-peaks, and his middle-ground has two swept ice rinks. Among the skaters and top spinners are five figures playing *eisschiessen*. Their five ice-sticks look bulkier than they were in later centuries, but the vertical central handles, with the correct *eisstock* tilt, are clearly seen; so too are the bands round the base, painted a lighter colour. His *Winter Landscape* would appear to be a Dutch scene, since no Alpine peaks are introduced. Village houses and a church are grouped around an ice pond with trees; flat, lightly wooded fields stretch away to a distant town. On the ice are two players with three ice-sticks, again with tall tilted handles on top. Although *eisschiessen* was a favourite national pastime in Bavaria and Austria,

20

Detail from Grimmer's *Winter*

and has spread in the present day to Switzerland, and even to
Wisconsin (Lake Okauchee), there is no record of its ever reaching
Holland. Bruegel would no more hesitate to incorporate it into
Dutch landscapes than he would Alpine peaks – just as he painted
Dutch scenes into Biblical subjects.

Another ice game, played in the Netherlands, was painted by
Bruegel's contemporary, Jacob Grimmer, in 1575. It is one of four
on the Seasons, titled *Winter,* and hangs in the Museum of Fine Arts
at Budapest. This painting has only recently been brought to curlers' notice by Bob Cowan of Glasgow, when he discovered a
reproduction, which he now owns. It depicts a curling scene not
dissimilar to a Scottish one. The composition bears some resemb-

lance to Bruegel's *Winter Landscape*: a frozen pond flanked by village houses with high roofs and a church spire, and by half a dozen trees, whose bare branches make arabesques against the sky. Beyond lies an open, snow-covered plain. Some thirty figures disport on the ice, some sliding, sledging, or whipping a top. At the far end, half a dozen players are gathered at each end of a short rink. The 'curling' blocks are not the *eisstock*. They are well rounded, fully as big as curling stones, but less squat and have no handles. The 'stone' in play is very large and white.

What were these 'stones'? Since none have survived in Holland, they may have been of wood, but more likely of ice or frozen snow as described under the word *kluyten* in Kilian's Germanic-Latin dictionary *Etymologicon Teutonicae Linguae* of 1632 and 1642. This dictionary was compiled by the Dutch philologist Cornelis van Kiel before his death in 1607. His name was latinized to Cornelius Kilianus for the first, Middelburg edition of 1620, which makes no mention of the word *kluyten;* this appears for the first time in the revised Utrecht edition of 1632, which renders it: *Ludere massis sive globis glaciatis, certare discis in aequore glaciato* – To play with frozen lumps or balls, to contend with quoits on a sheet of ice. In the 1642 Amsterdam edition, the revisers, while repeating the earlier definition, found the nouns *massa* and *globus* ambiguous; so they added the word *niveis* after *globis* – frozen snow-balls – and, to make *massis* clearer, added in French: *Louer à glaçons, ou monceaux de neige* – To play with blocks of ice, or of snow.

This may well be the game depicted by Grimmer, and his rink of only twenty feet would seem in accord; but one cannot jump to conclusions, for Bruegel's rinks were not any longer, although *eisstock* rinks are supposed to be at least sixty feet between hacks. Neither Bruegel nor Grimmer would allow trifles like that to upset the prior claims of composition. If Grimmer's players were throwing blocks of snow or ice, their game would not, like curling with stones, evolve. Nor did it. The game died without further trace. If the stones were real, then they must (from their bulk) have been far heavier than the Scots were able to throw without a handle, and that seems unlikely. A third game played on continental ice was the Scandinavian *knattleikr*. The earliest report was from Iceland in 1780, when Von Troil *(Letters on Iceland)* described it as 'playing with bowls on the ice'. It too died off and there is no record of its beginnings. There is nothing whatsoever to indicate that Scottish curling derived from any of these three.

22

The first known printing of the word 'curling' appeared in an elegy written in 1620 by Henry Adamson, a reader at the kirk in Perth. He had two close friends, James Gall, a merchant, and George Ruthven, a surgeon. When Gall died, Adamson wrote *The Muses Threnodie,* sub-titled *Mirthful Mournings on the death of Master Gall.* Scotland's first 'curling' comes in the first sentence of the preface: 'Anent the defunct, his name was M. James Gall, a Citizen of Perth, and a gentle-man of goodly stature, and pregnant wit, much given to pastime, as golf, archerie, curling; and Joviall companie.'

In the verses that follow, George Ruthven is given the part of chief mourner, who calls on his 'gabions' (chattels in a cupboard) to share in his grief. The inventory includes:

> His hats, his hoods, his bels, his bones,
> His allay bowles, and curling stones.

In a third reference, he reveals that the stones were collected from Lednoch (some four miles north of Perth):

> And yee, my loadstones of Lidnochian lakes,
> Collected from the loughs, where watrie snakes
> Do much abound, take unto you a part,
> And mourn for Gall, who lov'd you with his heart . . .

ANent the defunct, his name was *M. James Gall,* a Citizen of *Perth,* and a Gentle-man of a goodly ſtature, and pregnant wit, much given to paſtime, as golf, archerie, curling; and Joviall companie. A man verie kinde to his friends, and a prettie poet in liberall merriments, and tart ſatyres; no leſſe acquaint with *Philœnus,* and the *Acidalian* Dame, than with the Muſes.

From *The Muses Threnodie,* 1638

The casual use shows that 'curling' was a known word, needing no explanation. The *Threnodie* was published in 1638. That same year, the Assembly of the Church of Scotland met in Glasgow, when they accused Bishop Graham of Orkney of a heinous crime: 'He was a curler on the ice on the Sabbath day.' Incidental references of this kind appear at first rarely and then with increasing frequency in the Scottish records, but without detailed description of the game. In some parts it was not generally known as curling, but as coiting or kuting, and pronounced differently in different counties. In Ayrshire, some people called it coiting into the nineteenth century. For many of the common people of the land it was kuting until late in the eighteenth century, and only then did 'curling' oust it.

The very earliest stones were called loofies, from the Scots word loof, the palm of the hand. They were flat-bottomed and shaped like a hand, of around five-pound weight. From these, during the period 1500-1650, kuting stones were selected of heavier weight up to 25 pounds. Many specimens have been found in dried out or drained lochs and ponds. Some may have broken the ice on the throw and fallen through, but most had probably been left standing overnight on the rink, and been sunk by thaw – a later, frequent cause of loss. And some of these stones bear inscribed dates. The allegedly earliest is dated 1511 at Stirling. Others of more advanced kind, bored for handles, are dated 1551 and 1611. The more numerous, undated kuting stones, appear to be more ancient than these by far.

In no other country have such early stones been discovered, whether in lakes or houses, or outbuildings, or incorporated in walls, as they most certainly would have been had they existed. Nor were they reported by travellers, although Scotland's main foreign trade was with the Netherlands for two hundred years from 1540. A few researchers of Victorian times have suggested, basing their argument on Kilian's *kluyten*, that maybe the game was brought in by Flemish immigrants. That argument fails for the reasons given above; in addition to which, there was no introduction of curling to England, where most Flemings settled. The game then was Scottish in origin, as played on ice with stones.

It may well have antecedents in quoits. The words coiting and kuting strongly suggest this. Quoits appear to have been played on the Scottish and English borders since the fourteenth century, for it too was banned, by Edward III in 1349. The transfer of its simple principle – who can get a stone nearest a mark – on to ice would be a natural move, and the Middle English name *coyte* be borrowed. Moreover, the loofie game seems more akin to quoits than to curling.

The Scots took to winter kuting with something like alacrity. From around AD 1500 to 1700 the country was smitten by an oscillation of climate, which today's climatologists call the Little Ice Age. It brought the greatest cold since the Ice Age itself. While the Scandinavian glaciers advanced, the sea temperatures around Britain dropped at least 5°F below present temperatures – and these records were made eighty years after the maximum cold. In 1684 the river Thames bore eleven inches of ice. Eye witness reports

The nineteenth century winter was still severe enough.
Burns's Cottage, painted by Samuel Bough in 1876. It was Burns who immortalised in verse his old friend Tam Samson as a curler.

were of bitter summers, failure of harvests, and the wholesale destruction of woods. A huge expansion of Arctic pack-ice had occurred, with polar bears reaching Iceland. The British seas were frozen solid for some miles off shore in the winter of 1709. Since the frost went ten feet into the ground on that occasion, it can be imagined how solid the Scottish lochs froze. This – to look on the bright side of things – sounds like a curlers' winter paradise lasting two hundred years.

There were other good and practical reasons why the people of the country should then have taken to curling. The land was almost entirely agricultural and self-supporting in food-supply, yet almost all winter the ground was frozen, or at least not workable. Full provision for winter was made in autumn by the salting down of meat and fish in the barrel, and the storing of grain crops, but that done, work on the land stopped. The plough and spade lay 'frozen in the furrow'. I quote these last words from an old anonymous verse, which although doggerel like most curling verse, sums up the point to be made:

> The plow's froze in the furrow
> On barn roof lies the harrow,
> The trowel, spade and barrow
> Useless aside are cast.
> Save curlers there's few
> Who their faces dare shew,
> While 'midst frost and snow
> We are all in a glow.
> With our nimble brooms
> And our ponderous stones,
> Which smartly we ply
> Hard weather to defy,
> And thus we repel the blast.
>   Aghast!

A terser couplet on curling by a seventeenth century doctor, Alex. Pennycuick, reads:

> It clears the brains, stirs up the native heat,
> And gives a gallant appetite for meat.

An idle man soon becomes a trial to himself and his best friends. He has to be out and doing, and while the Scot has never lacked talent in thinking up ways to pass the time with enjoyment, in hard frost most ball games are out. Curling arrived opportunely, and although it was a minority game, earning no ban from kings and Privy Councils, it none the less enjoyed a quick spread from the Orkneys to the Borders. More surprisingly, because so many Scots had Norse blood, skiing had to wait the better part of four hundred years for its introduction from Norway in 1890.

A further incentive to curlers came of their poor housing in town and country alike, and the indoor cold and smell, which had to be countered by any vigorous exercise that would take a man out of doors, keep his circulation moving, and give his lungs fresh air. Even in Edinburgh, all the tenement buildings, six and seven stories high, were faced in wood during the sixteenth and seventeenth centuries. Few had glass in the windows. Shutters were ill fitting and the roofs thatched and leaky. Floors were as thick in dirt as the streets, and the indoor closets stank. Town houses were infested by mites. Since heating too was minimal, men of all ranks fled out of doors when they could, and some gladly took to curling on the Nor' Loch, which then covered the hollow under the Castle, where Princes Street Gardens now lie, or Duddingston Loch beyond the Salisburgh Crags.

Curling was more especially a country game, and beloved of the farmers. The surface of the Lowlands was very different from now. It was almost entirely destitute of trees, and even of bushes, except a few around the landowners' houses. There were no hedges and fences; all fields lay open, and since the people had not learned how to drain the land it was covered with lakes, marshes, and ponds, which have now long vanished. Travellers of the time reported in some surprise that the hillsides were sown with barley and oats to their summits, for so much of the low ground was too wet to bear crops. Since good curling ponds thus abounded, and hard weather was an annually reliable event, the other incentives had full play.

The country people of the east and central Lowlands, Southern Uplands, and Borders, had stone houses roofed in thatch or turf but without chimneys. The windows were only holes in the walls, stopped in storm with a straw bung or a cloth roll. In the Highlands, few stone houses could be seen apart from the clan chiefs'. They were almost all walled with turf. Thus Highlanders and Lowlanders alike suffered great temptation to hibernate in winter, and to 'red-den their legs by the fire' as one traveller recorded. The colder the weather the stronger the temptation, unless there were men of vigour around to winkle out the weaker brethren. Thus apart from the fact that curling was fun, it had in these times a most positive social value, and on more planes than one. The very change of environment from cold, smoky, smelly, ill-lit and uncomfortable houses to the crackling air and camaraderie of a curling pond was so beneficial to the spirits that one might wonder why, when the game spread so widely, it did not recruit faster – nearly two hundred years were to pass before the first clubs were formed, and nearly three hundred before a national body was founded.

Part of the reason is that Scotland had no roads, or at least none that could take wheels except within a few bigger towns, and not even there north of the Tay. The tracks were so rough that horsemen could travel no faster than walkers on a long journey, say from Edinburgh to Moray, which took a horse five days for a hundred and fifty miles. The post runners went on foot even from Edinburgh to Thurso. It followed that the countrymen were pro-digious walkers, and thought nothing of thirty to forty miles in a day, but maybe they baulked at loading themselves with stones. Com-munication, then, was slow and bad. Curlers were content to run their games within their own and nearby village communities as the weather allowed. There was no thought of organizing any game on more than this local basis, and no opportunity. All sports were, in the words of Government before the Reformation, and in the words of the Church after it, 'frivolous', except archery. The people too thought of them casually, and maybe enjoyed them the more. Competition in sport was no subject for serious planning.

Men were thus enjoying curling but under no pressure to improve it. The word 'competition' still held its original meaning: to strive together with others, rather than against others. There seems to have been no search for better stones in order to gain advantage over opponents. Any change had to come by slow degree. Since a player chose from river, shore and dyke whatever shape of stone took his fancy, it was gradually discovered that some performed better than others. The loofies were oblong and may at first have been thrown over the near part of the rink, like skiting a flat stone on water. The very first improvements made were the cutting of finger grooves and thumb holes to give better purchase,

28

and some smoothing of the sole for better glide. By the nature of the throw and the loofie's shape, it could be no part of the player's intention to give it a rotary motion, and so cause it to curl on the ice in order to 'draw' or curl round a guard stone. This advantage of a circular and heavier stone with a handle had to emerge by long process of trial at the beginning of the nineteenth century.

It should therefore be noted that the word 'curling' did not derive from the motion of a stone on its way down the ice, caused by imparting a spin. The true derivation has baffled researchers. It could be that it came from the old verb to curr – to make a low or hoarse murmuring sound – which would be the distinctive sound of a running loofie (just as the 'roar' is the sound of the heavier boulder). The insertion of the letter 'l' would be a natural adaptation to link the onomatopoeic verb to the game without confusing one with the other.

When heavier stones were chosen, the object was a more accurate delivery to the tee, furthered by using a fixed handle. The stone after a straight back-swing could be floored or soled near the forward foot – which meant also that a rotary motion could be given if wanted, and be controllable if the stone were round. This point was at first not appreciated. None the less, as the stones became rounder and heavier by a process of natural selection, the future growth of curling as a game of skill, and so for popular spread, would become for the first time possible. That was the opportunity offered to the Scots around 1650. The entire development of a local sport to a truly national sport depended then on the development of the stone itself, as the players discovered what could be done with it. How this happened is a more than useful study, for it goes to the very essence of the art. The important point to grasp is that the Scots did not so much 'invent' curling as evolve it – starting with a game that bears little likeness to curling as we know it today.

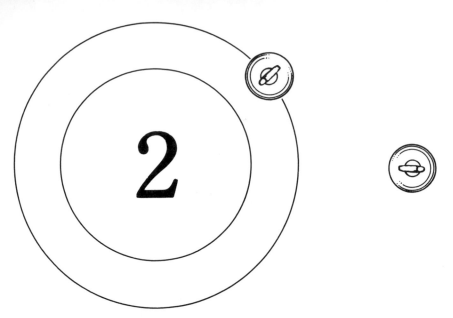

The Early Stones and Rinks: 1500-1800

The stones have evolved through three distinct forms: kuting stones; rough boulders with handles; and from the nineteenth century the round stone, which was finally refined into the beautifully shaped stone of today. These forms have no distinct dates. Their introductions heavily overlapped one with another, as might be expected when countryside communities lay so widely distant and out of ready communication. The periods may be loosely taken as kuting stones from around 1500 to 1650, and rough boulders from before 1650 to shortly after 1800.

The earlier stones were often called 'channel stanes', as well as 'loofies'. The first name presumably derived from that abundant source, the beds of burns, and then came to be applied to all water-smoothed stones, including sea-worn. The *loof* as noted earlier was the palm of the hand, and may have first been applied to the lighter stones chosen for a shape convenient to the hand for throwing somewhat in the fashion of quoits. In quoits the pins were 18 yards apart; the iron ring was pitched through the air. On ice the mark would lie at longer distance, and the throw be adapted by a swing at a narrow angle to the floor. The two games were on the face of it not so very different, but loofie-skimming had hidden

Three kuting stones. The top one has four raised bosses to enable it to run more smoothly.

potential for growth. The stones were as nature provided. The cutting of finger-grooves to give better grip allowed increase in weight, but the limitations imposed by shape and weight were severe. As much good chance as skill was needed to lie by the mark.

The Kuting Stones: 1500-1650

In the kuting stone period of one and a half centuries, weights varied from four or five pounds to twenty-five. The stones were gripped by means of a thumb-hole cut in the top of each stone and finger-grooves cut in the bottom. Some have survived, held in the posses-

The Stirling Stone, top and sole

sion of clubs, museums, ice-rinks, and private persons. They are generally four or five inches thick, and if one end is thinner the thumb-hole and finger-hollows are cut at the thick end.

Four early kuting stones are in the Smith Institute at Stirling. One, undated, weighs 15¾ lb, and like many others of the kind is an irregular triangle, but smoothly rounded. Its neighbour, Scotland's most famous stone, is dated 1511. There is no record of its history, but the rock from which it came is the basaltic lava on which Stirling Castle stands. It has a bluish tinge, weighs 26 lb and is roughly oblong, size 9 inches by 7½ by 4⅝. One face has the inscription A GIFT; and the other, St Js B STIRLING 1511. The thumb-hole is 1½-inch wide, and the finger-groove on the sole takes a 3-inch

curve. The initials may possibly refer to St James's Hospital (a
refuge for travellers) which at that time stood by Stirling Bridge.
The stone may well have curred down the rinks as early as the date
says, but the inscription is not in itself a proof. Men who claim
knowledge of engraving think that the stone was inscribed much
later. The date at least accords with the hospice, which disappeared
at the Reformation of 1560.

These and the large number of other kuting stones show clearly
the limitations on play. It was no game for women and children. A
man's strong hands were needed to grasp and throw the stone when
it approached ten pounds. In 1913, a practical experiment in throwing both kuting stones and boulders with handles was made at the

Throwing a loofie. The hand is that of Bob Cowan.

Crossmyloof Ice Rink in Glasgow. Two well-known curlers, A. Henderson Bishop and Bertram Smith, played a match with eight men a side as in early days, each with a single stone on a rink of thirty-five yards. They quickly found that the best method of delivery was to hold the kuting stone vertically, sole facing behind the tee, swing it back, and on the forward swing, which turned the sole from the vertical to the horizontal position, lay it down on the ice about two feet in front of the left foot. Bertram Smith reports that he found the soling so easy and effective that he felt it reasonable to suppose that this was how it was done four hundred years previously. The players found that the kuting stones ran keenly, but were most erratic in movement. The boulders, on the other hand, ran fairly true and many finished close to the tee.

That was on good indoor ice. On the less true outdoor ice, the kuting stone game must have embodied a large and frustrating element of chance. While weight gave a more estimable length on the rink, and a more accurate course, the rewards for any ordinary man would diminish if his kuting stone approached or exceeded twenty-five pounds. Only strong-arm men daily accustomed to outdoor work with their hands could play a stone of that order. This was the first sign of curlers seeking a team advantage from strength and weight. The handicap would be great for an opposing team that lacked them. Most likely the members of competing teams were balanced to allow for it. Every village or district had its own strong men, and the pairing of one with another in opposing teams would give a better game, add to the fun, and be in the tradition of the sport as handed down to succeeding generations. A better game still would be had by all if a handle were added to the kuting stone, allowing everyone the use of the heavier, steadier weight, with a much more accurate delivery. Yet a hundred and fifty years were needed for men to realize it. This was neither because they were stupid nor unenthusiastic, but because the climate of competitive sport was different from today's. Curlers seem to have been seeking not to develop new skills and tools, but simply to enjoy the fun of the game they had. They looked forward to enjoying it in the same old way next winter.

Boulders With Handles

Progress in a game as in any human activity is the work of a few individual men. In curling their names remain unknown, for they went unrecognized in their own times. The addition of a handle to a stone would hardly seem revolutionary. No one could foresee the far-reaching effects. Like kuting stones they were river-bed boulders, but not exclusively so, and were sometimes hewn by hammer and chisel to get reduction to the weight or shape wanted – at first some twenty pounds and upwards. More importantly they were each and all equipped with crude handles, many, perhaps most of them, of iron, for every village had its blacksmith. The handles were secured by running lead into bored holes. They were also made of wood, notably thornwood.

Handle-stones had become widespread after 1650, but were already appearing earlier in the century, and were not unknown in the sixteenth century. The earliest was found in a pond at Dunblane. It had two holes for the handle and bore the date 1551 (see Royal Club *Annual*, 1841). The stone was unhewn, just as it came from the river. Its find is perhaps more important than the 1511 kuting stone. If a handled stone had evolved as early as 1551, then how old must be the more primitive of early kuting stones? It seems hard to believe that curling was not prevalent in the fifteenth century.

Early handle-stones. That on the left shows evidence of having been shaped.

A long gap appears between this and the next dated handle-stone, engraved JM 1611. This one was found at Strathallan, when the foundation of an old house was being dug out at Loig in 1830. Its oblong shape had been chipped to better form by hammer. The initials and date had been deeply but crudely incised. Many other stones found undated were probably just as early, as judged by their similarity in size to kuting stones. Two specimens came into the hands of the marquis of Breadalbane in 1860, when a small loch near Tyndrum in Perthshire was being partially drained to make it safer for curlers. Both have handle-holes on top.

The signs are that the larger kuting stones were increasingly converted to handle-stones and the latter developed until all kuting stones had been finally driven out during the later seventeenth century. It may seem astonishing that they had lasted so long, but

Stone with three-legged handle. Dated 1700 and carrying the initials J.A. and M.W.H. it is believed to have belonged to Rev. William Halley, minister at Muthill, Perthshire.

37

the rough blocks with handles had just as long a run ahead of them. In this new period the name channel-stane, very commonly used for curling stones, refers mainly to the handled variety.

There was an immediate tendency for the channel stone to be thicker overall, if only to take the iron handle, which had to be deeply inserted and firm to take the weight and the swing. Apart from that, since the handles had been introduced to make twenty to twenty-five pound weights manageable, and to bring the advantage to everyone, further weight increase was inevitable. The river-smoothed stones with handles made possible a better stance for delivery, a smoother run down the rink, educed better broom work, and thus gave far greater accuracy over all in drawing, guarding, wicking, and the other skills. This undoubtedly happened, but the development of skills was for a long while inhibited, or delayed, by a too exuberant response to a challenge of another kind. It had already been seen with kuting stones how the heavier stones gained over lighter, and the strong arm over the weaker. Given handles, the strong men repeated the process, choosing heavier and heavier stones through the eighteenth century until, by its end, the move-ment had gone beyond all reasonable bounds, with stones reaching seventy and a hundred pounds and more. This was a blind alley, or more exactly, a needless detour, for the real challenge allowed by the handle-stone was overlooked by too many curlers. But not by all.

The new stones came in every conceivable shape. The triangular found favour with some – if struck on a tip by another stone it tended to birl on its bottom rather than move off the house, but square, rectangular, oblong, even conical stones were tried and apparently not found wanting. Every shape that a river could provide was there except the circular – which rivers provide most rarely. With skills in their use advancing, and each man selecting his own, and enthusiasm growing, more care was lavished by the fond owner on the choice and embellishment of his stone.

Something of the curling atmosphere of the eighteenth century and the way channel stones were fashioned is well illustrated in some verses by the Reverend George Murray. He was the minister at the small village of Balmaclellan at the head of Loch Ken in northern Kirkcudbrightshire, when he wrote seven stanzas in hon-our of his stone, which he had named *The Dean* (after the literary lion of the century, Dean Swift). The stone had been chosen from the Penkill Burn, which flows off hills of 2,300 feet into the river Cree:

> Where lone Penkiln, mid foam and spray
> O'er many a linn leaps on his way,
> A thousand years and mair ye lay
>   Far out of sight:
> My blessings on the blythesome day
>   Brought thee to light.
>
> Though ye were slippery as an eel,
> Rab fished ye frae the salmon wiel,
> And on his back the brawny chiel
>   Has ta'en ye hame,
> Destined to figure at the spiel
>   And roaring game.
>
> Wi' mony a crack he cloured your crown,
> Wi' mony a chap he chipped ye down,
> Fu' aft he turned ye roun and roun,
>   And aye he sang
> A' ither stanes ye'll be aboon
>   And that ere lang.
>
> Guided by mony a mould and line
> He laboured next with polish fine,
> To make your mirrored surface shine
>   With lustre rare –
> Like lake, reflect the forms divine
>   Of nature fair.
>
> A handle next did Rab prepare,
> And fixed it with consummate care –
> The wood of ebony so rare,
>   The screw of steel –
> Ye were a channel-stane right fair,
>   Fit for a spiel.

Ye had nae name for icy war –
Nae strange device, nor crest, nor star –
Only a thread of silver spar
      Ran through your blue;
Ilk curler kenned your flinty scar
      And running true.

A time will come when I no more
May fling thee free from shore to shore;
With saddened heart I'll hand thee o'er
      To some brave chiel,
That future times may here thy roar
      At ilka spiel.

In the eighteenth and nineteenth centuries, a channel stone was no inanimate object, and George Murray no exception in bestowing regard on his stone, and also a name, as though it had a personality of its own. On the rink it became a living thing. Regard was further concentrated by each man playing only one stone, and not a pair as later. No one might deny that each had an individuality of its own when shapes varied from the most rugged to the most elegant. Maybe an owner grew like his stone, at least when he came to the ice. Or maybe just chose his stone to fit his own character. Some were massy, to be hurled down the rink, scattering all before them by brute force, others of good proportion, of middle weight and well-rounded bottom, inviting if not yet receiving in delivery the in-turn or out-turn of the handle to beat the guards by a cunning curl instead of open force. Curlers knew their own stones, which like them had diverse qualities, were valued for them, and as need arose trusted to meet the rink situation in which they excelled. Since the rinks had eight players a side, most needs could be coped with by someone. The rinks must certainly have been well swept, with sixteen brooms at hand.

40

The first description of a curling match ever written was published in the *Weekly Magazine* of February 1771. The author was James Graeme, a divinity student, aged 22. The verse quoted is one of several:

> The goals are marked out; the centre each
> Of a large random circle; distance scores
> Are drawn between, the dread of weakly arms.
> Firm on his cramp-bits stands the steady youth,
> Who leads the game: Low o'er the weighty stone
> He bends incumbent, and with nicest eye
> Surveys the further goal, and in his mind
> Measures the distance; careful to bestow
> Just force enough; then, balanc'd in his hand,
> He flings it on direct; it glides along
> Hoarse murmuring, while, plying hard before,
> Full many a besom sweeps away the snow,
> Or icicle, that might obstruct its course.

The channel stone game could then, in many respects, have been no less interesting than now when stones are uniform. Players could not have the present-day skills or the same degree of satisfaction in using them, but the very diversity of stone-properties made up for that in added uncertainties, excitement, and surprise. There was certainly no less fun if much less subtlety. Each player had to know his stone intimately, and the care he lavished was natural, as George Murray makes plain. Handles became more ornate toward the end of the century, made in brass, bone, ebony, and even ivory and silver. Hours were spent honing and polishing the stones, which if not worshipped certainly had devotion.

The smaller stones still held their place, as witnessed by Thomas Pennant in his *Tour in Scotland in 1772,* when he visited Dumfriesshire. His is the second earliest and the most clear of all descriptions of how the game was played:

'Of the sports of these parts, that of *curling* is a favorite; and one unknown in *England*: it is an amusement of the winter, and played on the ice, by sliding from one mark to another, great stones of forty to seventy pounds weight, of a hemispherical form, with an iron or wooden handle at top. The object of the player is to lay his stone as near to the mark as possible, to guard that of his partner, which had been well laid before, or to strike off that of his antagonist.'

Although stones of 35 lb were not uncommon, it was the heavy stones that hogged publicity, and the names given are revealing: *Rob Roy* and *Bonaparte* (both much alive, at either end of the eighteenth century), *Wallace* and *The Baron* (88 lb), all surely the terrors of the rink. Others like *Bailie* and *Provost*, one might think to be fat and solid, not easily budged; or *Black Meg* and the *Grey Mare*, which would canter up the rink on drug ice. *Black Meg* was in fact a round stone of 66 lb and foreshadowed the coming of better shapes. *The Bible* sounds (and looks) like a thick heavy tome, not easily driven out from the inner circles. But the sound of a name was no sure guide to its properties, unless one knew why bestowed. *The Hen* turns out to be a Lochmaben stone of huge dimension, of which it was said, 'When once she settled, there she clockit.' And *The Egg*, which belonged to Perthshire's Blairgowrie team, was 115 lb. Their neighbours of Coupar Angus countered *The Egg* with *The Saut Basket*, 116 lb. The weight record goes to the County of

Jubilee, 117 lb

Berwick, which produced, it is said from the mouth of the Peas Burn near Cockburn's path, a stone of 117 lb, named *Jubilee*. It's earliest known owners were a family named Hood in the early 1800s. Like some monster of prehistoric times, it ended up as a museum piece, presented first to the Royal Caledonian Curling Club and now exhibited at Perth Ice Rink.

The young and brawny curlers required to lift the heavier stones off the ground, and sole them accurately, won a well-earned celebrity, if not dislocated discs. The real curling of the day was done with the forty to seventy pounders. The roar made by these channel stones on the ice was like a not too distant artillery barrage; their boom, it is said, reverberated off the moorland hills, quite unlike the muted sound on today's indoor rinks. To the curler's ear it was music, like the thunder of sea to a sailor's ear, or massed bag-piping to a Highlander's. The sound elevated the spirits, inciting deeds of prowess. Those handed down in the old records dwell on the more warlike.

The Lochmaben curlers tell the story of their president in the early years of the eighteenth century, who was challenged by Laurie Young of the neighbouring village of Tinwald to that ancient trial of strength – who could send a stone farthest. The two went to the Mill Loch, which was nearly a mile wide, to allow plenty of room for an unobstructed run. That loch must have borne the keenest of keen ice. The president threw first. He took a long back swing and then on the downswing managed to impart such power that his stone sped across the loch on and on, until a sharp eye was needed to see it. At last it struck the far bank with such force that it tumbled upward on to the grass. He turned to Laurie Young, 'Now you go across and throw it back, and we'll agree you're too many for us!' The wonder of the tale grows if we remember that the Mill Loch was unswept.

In justice to Lochmaben, it should be added that by the end of the century the parish was famed for its true curling skills. Its team of seven souters (cobblers) apparently knew so well, within the limits of their day, how to draw and wick and creep through the port, and how to strike their opponents' stones out of the house, yet temper force with canniness, that their opponents seldom or never gained a point. The term 'to souter' passed for long into curlers' language, meaning to win without allowing the other team to score at all.

The souters were finally defeated by the young Sir James Broun (father of Richard, the author of *Memorabilia Curliana Mabenensia*), who managed to raise a new local team of his own. 'It was a sad day for the Souters', said he 'and (for sorrow is dry) a wet night for them too.' Broun's team, from its long record of wins, became known in turn as the Invincibles.

Despite all their skills, the Lochmaben teams did not know how to make a stone curl round a guard by imparting a twist to the handle. That art required rounded stones, and these they did not possess.

A channel stone that was round enough to curl on its course, but which won fame for another reason, was Tam Samson's. It was a modest $54^{1}/_{2}$ lb, but he was the skip of the Kilmarnock rink after the middle of the eighteenth century, and one of Robert Burns's oldest friends.

It is virtually certain that Burns had taken to the rink. As a young ploughman and farmer in the counties of Ayr and Dumfries, both homes of the sport, he could hardly have lived there without curling on occasion. His friend Tam was wholeheartedly devoted to curling, and in summer to shooting over the moors. But the time came when he could no longer cope with the hills and hags, and had to lie on his long settle and listen to the tales of others. When a good yarn was told he would cry 'Hech, man! Three at a shot! That was famous!' At the close of his last wildfowl season, when he realised that he could not again go out, he said in a rash moment that he wished he were dead. When Rab heard this, he could not resist composing an elegy, and when Tam heard what he'd done he felt a little perturbed, and demanded that Rab read it to him. There were fifteen stanzas, each in praise of Tam's virtues and exploits. Two of them read:

> When winter muffles up his cloak
> And binds the mire like a rock;
> When to the loughs the curlers flock,
>   Wi' gleesom speed,
> Wha' will they station at the 'cock'? –
>   Tam Samson's deid!
>
> He was the king o' a' the core
> To guard, or draw, or wick a bore,
> Or up the rink like Jehu roar,
>   In time o' need;
> But now he lays on Death's 'hog-score' –
>   Tam Samson's deid!

44

Tam had a wry smile for the praises, but the fifteen times repetition of 'Tam Samson's deid' was too much for him. He exploded, 'I'm no deid yet, Robin! – I'm worth ten deid fowk!' The justice of the outburst moved Rab to try to make amends. He composed his *Per Contra*, which is now always printed at the close of the Elegy:

> Go fame, an' canter like a filly
> Thro' a' the streets an' neuks o' Killie;
> Tell every social honest billie
>   To cease his grievin;
> For, yet unskaith'd by Death's gleg gullie,
>   Tam Samson's leevin!

(Gleg gullie meant a sharp knife; the cock, the tee; and core, the body of curlers.)

One of a pair of stones from Meigle, Perthshire, known as the *Grannies.* None of those who took part in the experiment at Crossmyloof in 1913 was able to put Granny up the rink.

Tam in fact lived several years longer and died in 1795. A year later Burns was dead too.

Curling in the new century continued to produce many colourful characters. This was the transition period, when the virtues of the circular stone had already been discovered, news of it spreading, and the days of the channel stone numbered. At this very time the huge stones had achieved their greatest size, and the giants who could wield them their highest renown. John Cairnie, who was later to become first president of the Grand Caledonian Curling Club, gives a thumbnail sketch of two legendary heroes of his youth. He was at that time living in Stirlingshire, and writes:

'In our youthful days we often curled at night; fatigue was then unknown to us; we had a famous match on a sheet of water called the Drumlie meadow, near the village of Denny. . . . The most of us mustered on the ice before eight o'clock in the morning . . . (food) consisted of bread and cheese with porter *ad libitum*, and such of the company as chose had hot pints prepared consisting of porter, eggs, biscuit, sugar, and whisky, of a consistency as thick as ordinary porridge, and well might be called meat and drink; and although we partook freely of all the refreshments, we believe the whole party kept perfectly sober; at least none of them were so tipsy that they could not handle their massy gravities with the best effect:– and that they were massy cannot be doubted, as one pair weighed 72 lbs each stone. They were played by a very powerful man, named William Gourlay, who, at that time, we reckoned the king of curlers, and the execution done by them was most surprising, for when forcibly played full, they moved after taking off the guard and in their progress often raised half a dozen stones in succession, and gained the shot that was declared to be impregnable.'

His word 'execution' seems apt, for other eye-witnesses of the heavy-weights in action have reported that, when such a thunderer came down the rink, spectators had to scatter to evade split stones and flying chips. Split stones were perhaps not too serious a matter when the channel stones could be picked free from the burn. Since the stones were so rough and irregular, it is said that when the house had been built it looked as if a rock-avalanche had come to rest on the rink.

Cairnie goes on to describe an ambidextral giant named Aleck Cook. 'He had arms of extraordinary length, which he could swing so high with the curling stone behind him, that when about to raise the double guards, a person standing on the tee opposite could see its entire bottom.'

Cairnie's note on Cook is maybe apocryphal, yet true to the man in a general way. He continues, 'Several games were played, and it had been so arranged that every curler was to have a lanthorn and candle on the ice, which with the aid of a fine moon enabled us to continue the game till four o'clock in the morning, when, after emptying every bottle, or pint-stoup, we parted, much against the wishes of some of us, who would have preferred making out the 24 hours on the ice.'

These night-time matches were common enough throughout Scotland. Since the end of the Little Ice Age, long hard winters had been coming less frequently. Sometimes a few years had to pass between bonspiels. When a hard frost did come, it could no longer be relied upon to last as long as of yore, even though it might on a few occasions last for some weeks. Hence curlers felt under pressure to use every opportunity to the full. Who could tell when it might come again? So they curled by night if keen, and by day when the hill lochs were engulfed by mist, and when icy winds came out of the east, blowing spindrift. They no longer waited for so thick a build-up of ice. Reports of ice breaking under the curlers became more frequent without much deterrent effect, as witness the Fenwick skip who had just floored his stone on the forward swing, on the last throw of the game – when the ice collapsed under his feet. But the stone had safely left his fingers. While he went under his eye never left its mark. With only his head above water, chin on the broken edge, and thinking his last moment had come, he cried out as he saw his stone curl in to lie shot, 'Pit that yin on my heidstane!'

The Rinks

Despite such cautionary tales, curling was in good shape at the turn of the eighteenth century, and right on to the mid-eighties frosts came often enough (compared to now) to keep curlers in good heart. Big changes were brewing; the new stone was on its way, clubs forming, and the rink changing in length, markings, and accessory equipment.

Thus far, the rink had varied from thirty yards long to forty or more. There were no rules consistent for all Scotland. District teams agreed rulings best suited to themselves. Rink markings had since early days been introduced one by one as stones and play developed. In channel stone days, the tee circle or house, also called the brough or the boardhead, varied in diameter from two to twelve feet. Inner circles were inscribed only to help to measure shot distances from the tee. The tee itself was marked with a button, or a coin, or a pinch of snuff, and later with a small iron disc spiked into the ice. The player from the opposite foot-score was directed where to play by the skip, who stood behind the tee and placed his broom to show him where to aim; yet by the close of the nineteenth century some rinks began to mark the tee with a 'dolly', a foot high, shaped like a skittle – and still used on outside ice. The hog-scores (in some parts called collie-scores) were marked at a fifth or a sixth of the rink-length, and their lines drawn wavy to make them more easily seen against the cracks in the ice.

The players were generally seven or eight a side, but numbers could vary at extremes from four to twenty (the latter a rare occasion in 1841, in Kirkcudbrightshire), delivering one stone each, with a coloured wool tassel tied to the handle for quick recognition. Their game was usually a score of thirty-one shots. The earlier kuting and boulder stones had been delivered from a hack, notched three of four inches deep into the ice, but that could not have given a secure footing, nor could the hack be made without going through to water when winters grew less severe and thaws came sooner. Instead, to prevent foot-slip on delivery, spiked iron plates were devised for the feet and called crampits, cramps, or tramps.

Early crampits were strapped to the feet, and not to be confused with later crampits, which were lengths of sheet iron fixed at the foot-score. They were at first misused. Players walked all over the ice with them and ruined the rink until they were banned. Other iron plates were invented in the shape of crosses, triangles, and horse-shoes, one to hold the toes of the left foot, and the other the heel of the right; these were used only from the foot-score at the hack position. They were variously named as crisps, trickers, triggers, and grippers. These were the forerunners of the modern hack.

The brooms were almost invariably known as kowes. They were shaped like carpet switches. Since broom and willow were locally in short supply in the treeless Lowlands, until late in the eighteenth century, all kinds of twigs were pressed into service and tightly

bound. (Ayrshire curlers in dire straits had been known to flog the
ice with their Kilmarnock bonnets.) Since the kowe was nearly as

Curler, with crampits attached to his boots, and his kowe

A selection of trickers

important as the stone, almost equal care was soon to be given to its decoration – curved handles bound in silver, inscribed, and offered for competition as might silver cups in other sports. The way a broom could be revered for service given was rendered in verse last century by W. A. Peterkin:

My Bonny Broomy Kowe

In summers past I've seen thee bloom
   On mossy banks and knowe;
I've revelled mid thy sweet perfume,
   My bonny broomy kowe.
I've garlanded thy yellow flowers,
   I've lain beneath thy bough;
I'll ne'er forget thy youthful prime,
   My bonny broomy kowe.

You've been my friend at ilka spiel,
   You've polished up the howe,
You've mony a stane brocht owre the hog,
   My bonny broomy kowe.

50

As mem'ry noo recalls the past,
  My heart is set alowe,
Wi' moistened e'en I gaze on thee,
  My bonny broomy kowe.

Time tells on a'; your pith has gane,
  And wrinkled is my brow;
We're nae sae fresh as we hae been,
  My bonny broomy kowe.
You've wizened sair, and maist as thin
  As hairs upon my powe;
I doubt our days are nearly dune,
  My bonny broomy kowe.

When death comes o'er me, let my grave
  Be sacred frae the plough;
For cypress plant a golden broom,
  That yet may be a kowe.
Nor rest nor peace shall e'er be yours –
  A' curlers hear my vow –
Unless there grows abune my head
  A bonny broomy kowe.

    Sweeping became such a vital part of curling that players owning their own broom and stone were not content, as many are now at indoor rinks, to use any brush that lay to hand. The broom thus became as much an emblem of curling as the stone itself, as may be seen in group pictures of all ages. In channel stone days, sweeping could not be developed to the fine art of later times, when the round stone had evolved to draw it out of the players. The open air game on natural ice could make some heavy demands on sweepers other than their skills. As often as not, curlers arrived at pond or loch to find the ice blanketed in snow, which had to be cleared first with long boards (used like a snow-plough), or, if deep, dug with spades and then swept. In 1801, the Kilwinning team of Ayrshire turned out to find the rink covered overnight by a heavy snowfall, and no gear at hand to clear the worst of it. They stood by the brink in dismay. The day seemed lost – until one of their number, inspired by the spirit of curling, offered up his body in sacrifice. He proposed that his six foot length and heavy weight be used as a human rake. His team jumped into action. Shrouding him in his long plaid, which had ample cloth beyond head and foot to give them purchase, they dragged him back and forth across the rink until the brooms could be called in to whisk off what snow remained. The victim is named 'J.C.' in the records, and the joys of his martyrdom were for once of this world; the spirit neat and the heavenly music a roaring.

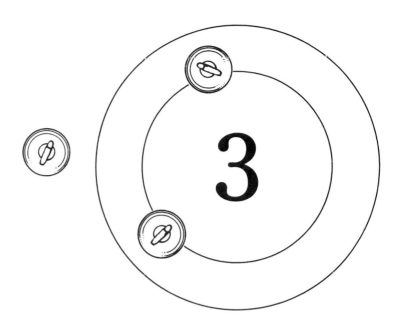

The Rise of The Clubs: 1700-1838

The evolution of curling had come about through the development of the stone, until around 1800; after that it came largely through development of the clubs. The channel stone curlers, after stravaiging through the long maze of great weights and diverse shapes, had as if by chance happened on the circular stone. From 1800, give or take a decade, the process of change became primarily a work of the clubs, in so far as it was they, organized, who could bring on the round stone to dominance, and then win the universal agreement on rules that allowed the competitive game to develop. Their nineteenth century role was to bring order out of a confusion to which they at first contributed. They provided a foundation for better days, when a governing body could be founded and curling become a truly national sport.

The First Growth

The clubs began to form through a real need. Throughout Scotland, the local players had casually assembled when the weather was right, dispersed when wrong, agreed on their own rules for play,

53

and fixed their own matches. A prominent part in arranging matches had also been taken by the landowners while they were still living on their estates, which at latest was up to the close of the eighteenth century (earlier in the Highlands). After that three-fifths or more were absentees in London or Edinburgh. Many had been enthusiastic curlers, encouraging one parish to challenge another, or one village another, and arranging bonspiels by challenge to a neighbouring estate owner and his tenants. But even this was spasmodic. Local teams rose and died too, some by loss of stones left out on the ice and sunk by thaw, or by emigration. While curling had never a wide spread in the Highland counties, it none the less had devotees all around the eastern and southern fringes, and within the Breadalbane and Atholl districts of Perthshire, and presumably in Inverness-shire, since Clan Fraser gave Canada its first curlers (1760) – all of which were affected by the replacement of cattle breeding by sheep farming, and the huge emigration that followed the Clearances.

The strongholds of curling were the Lowland counties, more especially of the south-west, and there too country populations were on the move, changing as a result of the Industrial Revolution, compounded with wars in France and America. The game itself was suffering, not only in the break-up of teams, but in disparities of play and rules and the confusions resulting. Clubs offered organization, records of play and tradition, communication one with another, and a continuing practice of curling.

There has been much controversy on which is the oldest club. The Kinross Club claims foundation in 1668. The important point is that no club system began to grow until the Kilsyth and Kirkintilloch Clubs were formed in 1716, followed by twelve more up to 1725. Growth was slow until after 1770, by which time the need was becoming urgent. By 1800 there were 42. In these thirty years great improvements had been made in the country's roads. There were still no railways.

The new clubs had much to contend with, in putting their own houses in order. Their members included some rugged individualists, and the broad social spread meant that rough characters were mixed in with the divines and the lawyers and the other professional men. It was a merit of curling that the game brought together every stratum of society, but a sample of their early rules shows that most clubs had learned the need to keep discipline.

Thus the Muthill Club of Perthshire in 1739: 'That there shall be no wagers, cursing or swearing during the time of the game under penalty of Two Shillings Scots for each oath. . .' (one imagines a rich harvest for club funds). Or the Sanquhar Club of Nithsdale, from minutes of 1782: 'Walter M'Turk, Surgeon, was expelled the society for offering a gross insult in calling them a parcel of damned scoundrels.' (But time honours the truthful, and he was reinstated later.) Or the Doune and Ardoch Clubs, whose rules bear a stamp of much experience: '(1) Only one member shall speak at a time . . . (2) Whisky punch to be the usual drink of the club in order to encourage the growth of barley. (3) No politics of church or state to be discussed. (4) No member to speak of the faults of another member in curling, nor deride office-bearers . . . (6) Any member who swears, dictates to another how to vote, or persists in trifling motions without being supported shall be fined. (8) The amount of each fine is to be 6d.'

Curlers' Courts were established wherever clubs were formed (with exceptions to the rule in the west). These were not to deal out justice, but to serve a still more basic function: to encourage the spirit of fraternity that made curling more than just a game. They had a *word* and a *grip*, and an initiation ceremony. The rest of a meeting-night was a frolic with horseplay, interrupted with a dinner of beef and greens. The Courts continue to the present day in the same spirit.

From ages past, beef and greens have been the traditional curlers' supper after play, whatever else may be added before and after. The bonhomie and big appetites, not to mention thirst, created by the game promised too much further enjoyment to be let go by a dispersal of players, if there was an inn or pub nearby. Such evenings could, in their own way, be nearly as memorable as events on the ice. Here are two verses from a member of the Duddingston Club; they re-create the conviviality of the brotherhood in *Cauld, Cauld Frosty Weather:*

> But now the moon glints thro' the mist
>   The wind blaws snell and freezing,
> When straight we bicker aff in haste
>   To whare the ingle's bleezing;
> In Curler Ha', sae bein and snug,
>   About the board we gather,

Wi' mirth and glee, sirloin the tee,
    In cauld, cauld frosty weather.

In canty cracks, and sangs and jokes,
    The night drives on wi' daffin,
And mony a kittle shot is ta'en,
    While we're the toddy quaffing.
Wi' heavy heart we're laith to part,
    But promise to forgether
Around the tee, neist morn wi' glee,
    In cauld, cauld frosty weather.

The Round Stone

Out of doors, the rules of the game, and members' opinions about stones and ways of play, were diverse enough to put brotherhood to the proof. During the last twenty years of the eighteenth century, round stones grew common, but the unshaped blocks dominated the rink to the closing years. Their phasing out was then under way, until, in the first quarter of the new century, the round stone had supplanted all others.

The coming of the round stone was a revolutionary event. Like most others in curling, before and since, it was not marked by immediate changes in play. The revolution had taken a long time to come and would take a long time to achieve its effects. Since curlers still owned their own stones, made to their own specifications, they had no uniformity. Some were most uncouth; weights varied from 26 lb to 75 lb. There could be no equality of play in a match between owners of heavy stones and those with lighter. If the ice were keen, the heaviest won; if drug or damp; the lighter won. To complicate matters, several clubs were experimenting in new varieties of sole.

Curlers all had their own ideas on the best rock for a stone. Ayr took pride in its stones of best Ailsa Craig granite, while Kilmarnock, only twelve miles up the road, damned them with faint praise and preferred dark blue whinstones from Sanquhar in the Nithsdale Hills, or *Burnocks* of light blue-grey rock speckled white from the Burnoch River of Ayrshire. Other clubs or teams chose *Crawfordjohns* from the uplands of Lanarkshire, or *Blantyres* from the Clyde Valley, or *Carsphairns* from the hills of Kirkcudbrightshire, or *Crieffs* from Perthshire, and many other stones from other places.

The blocks were picked up from the fields and hills, from the bottom row of dykes, from the rivers and sea-shores, and from the shore of Ailsa Craig ten miles off Girvan, on the Firth of Clyde, whence they were ferried to Ayrshire ports.

The curler's first step, in choosing his stones, was to be sure that the raw blocks were free of any crack; otherwise the long labour of shaping the stones could be lost. The method of ensuring sound-

Rounded stones with 'looped' handles. This style of handle appears to have been more common in Stirlingshire and Perthshire than in the rest of Scotland.

Pair of single-soled stones with wooden handles

ness, as recommended by Sir Richard Broun of Lochmaben in 1830, was to place them overnight in water, and next day expose them either to hot sun or an open fire. As the blocks dried, any crack would show up clearly as a wet seam.

The boulders were next hewn into perfectly round stones by a local mason, to a weight and shape approved by the owner. Some preferred a flattish stone, others a high. The diameters chosen were ten to eleven inches, and the heights $4^1/_4$ to $5^1/_2$ inches. Each sole was very gently rounded to the edge, so that it ran not on its whole diameter of apparently seven or eight inches, but on the lesser inner circle that made actual contact with the ice, which might be two or three inches, and less or more as the owner prescribed.

The polishing of the stones was of prime importance. Any curler who had the chance to test the soles on ice before and after was sure of a big surprise. The method of polishing was first to hone the bottoms with a sharpening stone from the bed of the river Ayr. A few minutes hard honing had the same effect on a stone's running, said Broun, as it would on the shaving power of a blunt razor. The bottoms of the stones were then heated before a strong fire at some distance, and gradually moved closer to extract all damp. Linseed oil or tallow was then brushed on repeatedly until the stones could absorb no more; after which, they were gradually withdrawn from the fire to allow cooling by slow degrees. When cold, they were immersed except for the soles in buckets of water, and exposed to a night of frost. Finally, all external oil was removed by honing in warm water. It seems not possible, now, to know if Broun's practice was peculiar to Dumfriesshire.

Handles were given distinctive shapes, and inserted at whatever

The handle of this rounded stone is at an angle instead of being, as was usual, along the diameter of the stone, perhaps as an experiment to aid 'twist'.

angle the owner wished. Some liked them parallel to the top, others tilted at an obtuse angle; some liked the stone pierced at centre, others more to the side. And the cost of such a stone complete with its brass handle was in 1830 one guinea at most. (A labourer's wages were a shilling a day, and a good stone was the price of a Cheviot ewe.)

The Years of Experiment

From 1800 to 1838, the rise of the clubs coincided with a remarkable stimulation of practical experiment, both in equipment and technique. Members were more active in this field than ever before in the history of the game. The clubs, better road communication, and more inter-parish competition, interacted in achieving this stimulus – as also in opening curlers' eyes to the general state of confusion in practice, and the need to standardize rules and equipment. Before that happened, innumerable ideas were tried out and experiments made, adding their quota to the ferment. The curling pot was on the boil. Among the worse ideas, which were thrown out in due course after distillation of the better, were broad soles of seven- and eight-inch diameter; a stone running on a one-inch central circle, developed and approved by Wishaw Club, who also experimented with stones running on three rounded stumps, each $1/8$ of an inch in length; and steel bottom-linings, tried and approved by Beith and Dalry Clubs in face of all opponents' objections. These and a score of other innovations ended up on time's midden. But some came through the distillation process, refined, and are recognizable now, even if not in the 1830s, as evolution's pure malt. They had to stand in the cask, as it were, maturing for long years until curlers took to them. They were the concave sole, the twist, the reversible handle, and the artificial rink.

The Concave Sole

The Fenwick Club, near Kilmarnock, made concave soles and tried them out in the early 1800s. In this experiment, they had taken up for re-trial a sole first made at Hamilton as early as 1784. The stone ran on the cup-like rim – now the universally approved design. Fenwick, perhaps too hastily, decided not to continue them because, they said, the bottoms collected debris, and 'they can

Wicker baskets used to carry curling stones in the nineteenth and
early twentieth centuries. The handle of the stone was now in the
centre and was reversible.

never be made to run perfectly true, and are worse than flat-
bottomed stones from their being turned from their course by every
obstruction.' Their rejection may have been made from a trial on
white ice with a rough or biassed surface, or been due to faultily
made rims. The concave sole came into its own in the last decade of
the century, after its adoption by Canada.

The Reversible Handle

Until 1800, nearly all stones had their handles fixed off-centre. In
the first quarter of the century, several clubs made the experiment

61

of piercing their stones right through the middle, and so allowing the handle to be bolted to either side. One side could thus run on a five- to seven-inch sole for keen ice, and the other on a three- to four-inch sole for drug ice. A great advantage could be gained on outdoor ice by this reversion of sole, but some curlers disliked double bottoms, they said, because the hole tended to collect dirt or granules, thus impeding the stone. The reversible handle came into general use in the 1880s, at which time the concave sole joined it.

The Twist

The round stone had brought great opportunities for development of the game. One was to make the stone at the end of its path curl several feet in or out by imparting a turn to the handle. The secret of this skill had been discovered at least as early as 1784, at the time of a match at Lochwinnoch between a Castlesemple team and one raised by the duke of Hamilton. The following lines were then written, and record a tense moment, for a thousand guineas had been staked on the game (most unusually):

> Six stones within the circle stand,
> And every port is blocked,
> But Tam Pate he did turn the hand,
> And soon the port unlocked.

The secret remained a secret until the young curlers of Fenwick rediscovered it in 1800. When the stone is leaving the hand, and the handle is given a turn inward, the stone will be made to rotate clockwise. At the end of its slide, when the rotation is slowing down, the sole bites more on the ice and the stone curls rightwards. An out-turn rotates the stone anti-clockwise and gives a final left-ward curl to the mark. Fast spin means less draw. A rotation of three times or fractionally more between backline and tee gives most draw. The value of the twist – now called 'in-turn' or 'out-turn' – in curling round a guard to lie by the tee, or striking out a stone, can be seen at once on today's good indoor ice. But that was not so last century. The Fenwick players extolled the skill; most others were sceptical, and saw it only as a possibly useful device for countering a bias on the ice. Outside ice can often be slow and warped, and calls for more strength than delicacy, therefore not giving the master of the twist much advantage.

The evolution of the curling stone. Clockwise from left – a 'loofie':
channel stane with iron handle, *The Egg,* 115 lb: hammer-dressed
single-soled round stone: modern indoor stone of Welsh Trevor.

The Fenwick twist provoked opposition, not because other curlers knew nothing of it, but because they did, without knowing quite
enough. Even John Cairnie of Largs, who later became first president of the Grand Caledonian Curling Club, scorned the practice:
'When twisting or turning the handle becomes necessary from
biasses on ice that is water-borne, we think the game comes to be
entirely a game of chance. It must, however, even on the best ice,
be an uncertain method of gaining the end. We apprehend straight
lines are those that should be studied by the curler, or if the advance
in the science of twisting be such as to render it as certain as the play

in general use, we are of opinion that ice-bowling may come to rank amongst our winter amusements.'

The clubs' initial doubts were laid to rest in the 1880s, when the controlled twist was accepted by all as a needed skill, although not then as a basic – that is, one without which games could not be won.

Equipment

The round stone brought one quick change in play tactics. Redding the rink was no longer esteemed. There was growing emphasis on canny play, drawing and guarding and building up a house. That, in turn, drew closer attention to sweeping. Kilmarnock voiced near-heresy by declaring the broom-kowe obsolete: they now chose hair brooms of the kind used for sweeping house-floors, and swore by felt-soled shoes for enjoyment of free movement over the rink.

A minority of curlers still delivered the stone wearing the old-style barbarous crampits strapped to the feet. John Cairnie had been experimenting, and now introduced his new crampit of sheet iron, frosted on both sides and stuck on at the foot-score without need of spikes. Some clubs preferred wooden foot-boards.

Rink lengths had settled down to between 40 and 49 yards, which still allowed plenty of room for dispute. While most clubs continued to field rinks of seven or eight men playing one stone each, several by the 1830s were preferring four players a side with two stones each, and stones were introduced to the rinks in roughly matched pairs. This was to prove the winning practice; it gave a better, more satisfying game.

Artificial Rinks

A landmark in this period of change was John Cairnie's artificial rink, made in 1827. Frosts of any length were by the early nineteenth century less frequent than could satisfy the abounding enthusiasm of round-stone curlers. John Cairnie, living on relatively mild country at Largs, took thought. He had noticed, like most curlers, that shallow ponds froze faster than deep, and at higher air-temperatures. Unlike others, he acted by trying to make an artificial rink. He remembered well as a boy making instant slides on street pavements by throwing on water in frost. So why not for curling? His first effort in 1813 lapsed when he found he could not raise enough money. The second and successful attempt to make the world's first artificial rink was completed in January 1828. Cairnie

Cairnie's Pond at Curling Ha', from an oil painting

built his rink on his own grounds of Curling Hall (on the site of the Battle of Largs, where the Scots in 1263 had fought off King Hakon of Norway). The rink was of clay and whinstone chips rolled flat. Frost came a day or two later, when he flooded the rink with a quarter-inch of water. It froze overnight and next day gave perfect curling to a party of eight.

Better still, he found that ice fit for curling could be had in a few minutes by sprinkling water from the rose of a watering-can. It formed ice on the instant, and only a few coatings were needed. Hopes of cheap, quickly made rinks ran high, but Cairnie had forgotten the gardener's friend, the worm. Its holes leaked out the water and couchgrass broke the surface. The rinks had to be remade with lime, sand, and stone, on which paving stones were laid with their joints sealed by mastic.

At much the same time as Cairnie, the Reverend Dr Somerville of

Currie had invented a similar rink with a pavement floor. There was some dispute as to who was first; the award has by general consensus gone to Cairnie, but Scottish curlers were indebted to both men – as always, without fully knowing how much at the time. The paved rink allowed good curling when other ponds had none, yet only a few clubs or men followed the Cairnie-Somerville lead in the next twenty years. Perhaps curlers felt reluctant to introduce any kind of artificiality into a sport so closely bound to the natural elements for so many centuries. As for artificial ice-making, which came later in the century, that would have evoked anathema in the 1830s.

The Clubs and Their Members

When clubs and teams met on the ice, and office-bearers corresponded, the wish for more uniform practice grew powerful, especially on rink-lengths and stone-weights, and the rules of play itself – some players, for example, if they were wearing strap-on crampits, could not resist stepping sideways along the foot-score to get a better line past a guard. But who was to give rulings for the game on occasions where a local team felt so convinced of its own right as to seem thrawn to its neighbour? And in the wider field – the good of the game itself – what practices were best encouraged or supressed? A governing body was needed.

Meantime, the clubs coped as best they could with their own delinquents. Worse crimes were recorded than side-stepping at the foot-score. John Cairnie writes of some incidents (not comic at the time): 'We have witnessed more than one attempt at foul play by some of our opponents who, when hard pressed, have had recourse to the base expedient of dropping snipe-shot before the stone coming up: and, in this way, of very soon stopping its progress.' Most tantalisingly, he fails to say what happened next.

Such incidents were exceptions to the general rule of fair play. The Reverend Henry Duncan of Ruthwell, Dumfries, wrote in these same years some poetry that excellently conveys the spirit of the game and the heady atmosphere of a bonspiel. Its concluding prayer is, incidentally, a peculiarly apt grace for a beef-and-greens dinner.

The Music of the Year is Hushed

The music of the year is hushed
  In bonny glen and shaw, man,
An' winter spreads o'er nature dead,
  A winding sheet o' snaw, man;

O'er burn and loch the warlock frost,
  A crystal brig has laid, man,
The wild geese, screaming wi' surprise,
  The ice-bound wave ha'e fled, man.

Up, Curler! leave your bed sae warm,
  And leave your coaxing wifc, man,
Gae, get your besom, trickers, stanes,
  And join the friendly strife, man;
For on the water's face are met,
  Wi' mony a merry joke, man,
The tenant and his jolly laird,
  The pastor and his flock, man.

The rink is swept, the tees are marked,
  The bonspiel is begun, man;
The ice is true, the stanes are keen;
  Huzza! for glorious fun, man;
Hush! no' a word – but mark the broom,
  And take a steady aim, man.

Here draw a shot – there lay a guard,
   And here beside him lie, man,
Now let him feel a gamester's hand,
   Now in his bosom die, man.
There fill the port, and block the ice,
   We sit upon the tee, man;
Now tak' this inring sharp and neat,
   And mak' the winner flee, man.

How stands the game? It's eight and eight:
   Now for the winning shot, man,
Draw slow and sure, the ice is keen,
   I'll sweep you to the spot, man.
The stane is thrown, it glides alang,
   The besoms ply it in, man,
Wi' twisting back the players stand,
   And eager, breathless grin, man.

A moment's silence, still as death,
   Pervades the anxious thrang, man,
Then sudden bursts the victors' shout,
   Wi' hollas, loud and lang, man;
Triumphant besoms wave in air,
   And friendly banters fly, man,
Whilst, cauld and hungry, to the inn,
   Wi' eager steps, they hie, man.

Now fill a bumper to the brim,
    And drink wi' three times three, man,
May Curlers on life's slippery rink
    Frae cruel rubs be free, man;
Or should a treacherous bias lead
    Their erring steps agee, man,
Some friendly inring may they meet
    To guide them to the tee, man.

The outdoor game in natural surroundings inspired curlers with memories more vivid than is possible after play on an indoor rink.

Contemporary illustration for James Fisher's *A Winter Season,* 1810. Fisher was blind, and his description of a game of curling in verse rhythm is notable for his expression of the sounds that are heard. There is however no historical evidence for the completely hemispherical shape that his artist gave the stones.

Time and again they were moved to express it in verse, most fortunately for us, for the poets were more perceptive than others. The following lines are from verses by David Gray in 1820, after a day with the Waterside curlers of Kirkintilloch, Dunbartonshire:

> . . . And oh, the journey homeward, when the sun,
> Low-rounding to the west, in ruddy glow
> Sinks large, and all the amber-skirted clouds,
> His flaming retinue, with dark'ning glow
> Diverge! The broom is brandished as the sign
> Of conquest, and impetuously they boast
> Of how this shot was played – with what a bend
> Peculiar – the perfection of all art –
> That stone came rolling grandly to the Tee
> With victory crowned, and flinging wide the rest
> In lordly crash! Within the village inn,
> What time the stars are sown in ether keen,
> Clear and acute with brightness; and the moon
> Sharpens her semicircle; and the air
> With bleakly shivering sough cuts like a scythe,
> They by the roaring chimney sit and quaff
> The beaded usqueba with sugar dash'd.
> Oh when the precious liquid fires the brain
> To joy, and every heart beats fast with mirth
> And ancient fellowship, what merry grasps
> Of horny hands o'er tables of rough oak!

Celebrations like these were not always the order of the day, or night. When curling weather came, the game could seize men like a mania, causing them to stay off work and neglect bread-winning duties. The weavers of Lochwinnoch, in 1829-30, were thus unable to resist the fascinations of the rink, and the frost lasted too long – too long at least for their sorely tried wives and families. Andrew Crawfurd of that village records how one wife made her point. Her man had come in expecting to be fed, and finding the table bare and himself kept waiting, made complaint and cast an impatient look at her food-cupboard. At this, 'She assumed a blithe look and bade him keep up his spirits till supper. She bustled, set a table, knife and fork; and when supper came, lo! it was a curling stane.'

The trades-folk were not the only offenders in elevating curling above work. The ministers of the kirk did not always set their flock a better example. In 1745-46 there was a most long and severe frost, when the Reverend Dr Wotherspoon of Beith came often to Lochwinnoch for long days on the ice, followed by nights at Strand's Inn. One Saturday night, he and his friends were still there as the Sabbath drew close. Strand's wife, a devout church-goer, thought he must have forgotten the hour and whispered in his ear a hint of his next day's duty. He dismissed the warning in a confidential aside: 'A minister,' said he, 'who can't shake a sermon out of his coat sleeve is a silly coof.'

The Lord heard him. Retribution came swift. Thus far the people on the south side of the loch had been able to walk across it to kirk on thirteen successive Sundays. But now the burns dried up, and with no water coming into the loch the ice buckled and went to the bottom. There was no more curling at Lochwinnoch. A nice finishing touch was put to this unhappy scene by the record, 'At funerals, people's nose-drops froze like shuckles' (husks of corn).

Curling was not only a countryman's game. Glasgow by 1825 had eight clubs, and Edinburgh four with nine more close around in the Lothians. The two cities had in fact more than these, although not officially instituted as clubs, and some were at the outskirts in what were still rural villages. An example is Partick in Glasgow, where the club's members (after its formal founding in 1842) used to meet for their beef and greens in Mrs Sinclair's tavern. The pub was then the only building in what is now that busy thoroughfare, Byres Road. It still stands today. The pre-eminent club of Scotland was the Duddingston Club of Edinburgh. Its one hundred and sixty-odd members included many of high social and professional rank, culled from all parts of Scotland. More pertinently, they had a far-seeing regard for curling and the will and position to foster it. The game had been played there since early times and prospered in status. By ancient custom, the provost and magistrates used to open the curling season by marching in procession with bands playing, both to the Nor' Loch before it was drained in 1780, and to Canonmills.

Duddingston Club was formed in 1795. Its rules came surprisingly close to those of the present day. For example: rink-length to be 36 to 44 yards, or else as agreed by the players; the hog-score to be one sixth of the length from the tee; each player to foot in such a manner that, in delivering his stone, he brings it over the tee; all curling stones to be circular; none of the players, upon any oc-

71

The Curlers as it is today

casion, to cross or go upon the middle of the rink; and so on. The only odd exception was the ruling that the player's party might not sweep his stone until it had passed the farther, not the nearer, hog-score. The important points were: (1) they insisted on round stones, and made war on multiform boulders when that influence was most needed; (2) they discouraged the thirty-yard rink. These two points won their way during the next thirty years.

Such progress was not easy going. Scotland's curlers were conservative, perhaps because they loved the old game so well. Any changes had to be long scrutinized before approval could be given, and no rule admitted that could not be seen to be needed. The auld channel stane, for all its faults, could not be displaced in a day, as James Hogg, the Ettrick Shepherd, made plain:

The Channel Stane

Of a' the games that e'er I saw,
Man, callant, laddie, birkie, wean,
The dearest, far aboon them a',
Was aye the witching channel stane.

> Oh! for the channel stane!
> The fell gude game, the channel stane!
> There's no a game that e'er I saw
> Can match auld Scotland's channel stane.

I've played at quoiting in my day,
And may be I may do't again,
But still unto myself I'd say,
This is no the channel stane.

Were I a sprite in yonder sky,
Never to come back again,
I'd sweep the moon and starlets by,
And beat them at the channel stane.

We'd boom across the milky way,
One tee should be the Northern Wain,
Another, bright Orion's ray,
A comet for a channel stane.

The Ettrick Shepherd was president of the Ettrick Club, but also a member of Duddingston, and thus subject to its liberal influence – or as James Hogg might have thought, radical influence. By 1825, boulder stones had become antiquities, except in the more remote parts of the country. Duddingston even looked forward to the day when Edinburgh might have an artificial rink. The more immediate and pressing need was for uniformity in the rules, the number of stones allotted to each player, the number of players to each team, the size of the stones, and the length of the rink. In the 1820s and 1830s, dispute on such points disrupted the county bonspiels between Midlothian, Peebles, and Lanarkshire. If the game were to become a national sport, and its brotherhood preserved, a national body had to be formed.

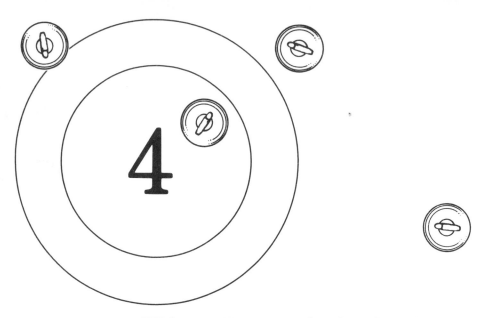

The Royal Caledonian:
1838-1888

The initiative in founding the Royal Caledonian Curling Club can be attributed to no one man, for several were involved, and one was of unknown name. But, if the delivery of the club might be likened to that of a curling stone, then it was John Cairnie who swung it down the rink and gave it handle to curl round a guard. That guard had been previously laid by Sir Richard Broun, and dubbed by him *The Amateur Curling Club of Scotland*.

John Cairnie was in bodily stature not like the heroes of his youth, with whose feats he regaled curlers later. He was comparatively slight in build, but strong in personality. Born at Dunipace in Stirlingshire around 1769, he qualified as a surgeon in 1792 and joined the East India Company, with whom he served at first in Ceylon and then in the 2nd Madras Native Cavalry. He lost his left arm in a gunpowder explosion. The practice of surgery now being closed to him, he retired to Scotland in 1805, married, and in 1813 built Curling Hall at Largs. Being the man he was, he took retiral at thirty-six as an opportunity for renewed life. He sailed in summer and curled in winter.

Twenty years later, when he wrote and published his *Essay on Curling* (1833), he mentioned that Sir Richard Broun had suggested

John Cairnie, a contemporary engraving

founding an Amateur Curling Club, and added, 'We think it would be a very desirable matter that, connected with this Curling Club, it should be recommended that every curling society in Scotland should correspond and give in a list of their office-bearers, the number of curlers, matches played, and any matter connected with the game that is interesting.' Clearly he had in mind a club that united all curlers.

Broun had in mind something quite different. He had given a valuable service to curlers in 1830 with the publication of his *Memorabilia Curliana Mabenensia*. Its title was perhaps an augury of the ideas he might have about a national club, suggesting as it does (although without conscious intent) that his book was not for the common herd. In the year after Cairnie's encouraging comment, Broun's proposal came out. Under the heading *Prospectus*, he announced the 'Amateur Curling Club of Scotland, instituted 1834, For Promoting and Cherishing the Noble and National Game of Curling'. So far so good, but his second proposition cut the legs from under the first. It read: 'That the Amateur Curling Club shall be entirely exclusive, embracing the names of such curlers alone as are entitled to be handed down to posterity as associated with the ice of the nineteenth century.' More followed in the same vein.

Who were these curlers, whose names could be handed down? Broun's preliminary list removed doubt. He nominated four dukes, an earl, two lords, and two baronets, all to take the chief offices, with the Ettrick Shepherd and several others as secretaries. In striking contrast to the social camaraderie of the curling rink, this society appeared to leave no room for Lochmaben souters, even if they were invincible, or for the young dairymen and weavers of Fenwick, even if they were pioneers of in-turns and out-turns of the handle. His new club broke up at the launching. It foundered without trace. No one wanted a club hostile to the spirit of the game, to its centuries-old origins, traditions, and chance of growth.

The club that everyone wanted, but seemed for a while to despair of having, was one to unite all curlers in brotherhood. In the spring of 1838, a pamphlet was published in Edinburgh titled *Laws of Curling*, written by Dr George Walker Arnott of the Orwell Club (Loch Leven). He probably felt exasperated by the prevalent lack of law. He noted that while brother curlers had much the same *grip*, they differed as to *word*, and urged that the initiated clubs get together to solve the problem. His suggestion was promptly fol-

> **T**O CURLERS.—In consequence of an advertisement
> which appeared in the North British Advertiser of 26th May 1838,
> a MEETING of CURLERS was held in the Waterloo Hotel, on the
> 20th inst., JOHN CAIRNIE, Esq. of Curling Hall, Largs, in the Chair.
> Deputations from various Clubs appeared, who approved generally of
> adopting a uniform set of Regulations, applicable to the whole of Scot-
> land, assimilating the technical terms, forming a court of reference, &c.
> But anxious for a fuller representation of the different Clubs through-
> out the country, in order to perpetuate and connect more closely the
> Brotherhood in this Ancient National Game, they Adjourned to WED-
> NESDAY, 25th of JULY NEXT, at twelve o'clock, in the Waterloo Hotel,
> when they hope the different Clubs of Scotland will make a point of
> sending Deputations.   JOHN CAIRNIE, Chairman.

lowed by some unknown curler, who placed this notice in the *North British Advertiser* of 26 May:

'To Curlers. – In consequence of what is suggested at p. 11 of the "Laws of Curling" (a pamphlet just published by Maclachlan & Stewart, Edinburgh), it is hoped that the Initiated Curling Clubs in Scotland will depute one of the Brethren of their Court to meet in the Waterloo Hotel, Edinburgh, on Wednesday, the 20th June next, at 11 o'clock a.m., for the purpose of making the mysteries more uniform in future, and if requisite, to form a Grand Court, to which all provincial ones shall be subject, and to elect a Grand President, with other Office-bearers. It is hoped that all Brethren who see this notice will direct the attention of the President or Secretary to it without delay. – 16 May 1838.'

On the day appointed, barely a dozen curlers turned up for the meeting. The clubs had declined to move for an unsigned adver- tisement, with an agenda limited to the 'mysteries', and probably bore in mind their experience of the Amateur Club, which still sat on their hopes like an incubus. The more optimistic dozen, meeting at the Waterloo, waited for the advertiser at first with some surprise at his absence, and then, when it became plain that he was not coming, with a strong sense of disillusionment. No one had come prepared in mind for such a dénouement. No one would take the leadership. The meeting was about to break up, when a small man of resolute bearing walked through the doorway. An empty sleeve of his frock-coat was pinned to his left breast. He presented his card, and with a blunt but genial manner declared his name as John Cairnie of Curling Hall, Largs. As soon as he had heard and assessed the situation, he took over the meeting. No one there knew him. His personality was dominating, yet everyone liked him instantly. He was promptly elected chairman. The meeting agreed on their broad aims, but rightly felt that their numbers were too few to be representative of Scottish curlers, and that a new meeting would have to be called on a properly signed, better advertised notice – and one with a broadened agenda. This was prepared and entered thrice in the *Advertiser* (the first on 23 June).

'To Curlers – . . . . a MEETING OF CURLERS was held in the Waterloo Hotel on the 20th inst., John Cairnie Esq., of Curling Hall, Largs, in the chair. Deputations from various clubs appeared, who approved generally of adopting a uniform set of regulations applicable to the whole of Scotland, assimilating the technical terms, forming a Court of Reference, etc. But anxious for a fuller representation of the different clubs throughout the country in order to perpetuate and connect more closely the Brotherhood in this Ancient National Game, they adjourned to Wednesday, 25th July next, at 12 o'clock, in the Waterloo Hotel when they hope the different clubs of Scotland will make a point of sending deputations.

John Cairnie, Chairman'

On 25 July, 44 curlers appeared in name of 36 clubs. They were found to give a wide scatter of membership across Scotland from the Borders to the Tay, and from the Firth of Clyde to the Firth of Forth. This meeting was representative. It could act. Dr Renton of Penicuik formally proposed, 'That this meeting do form itself into a club composed of the different initiated clubs of Scotland under the name of the Grand Caledonian Curling Club.' The motion was unanimously carried and John Cairnie elected first president.

Cairnie had taken forethought. After providing for the drawing up of a constitution and rules, he had arranged that the members stay on for a Curlers' Court and dinner. The Club's *Annual* (year book), soon to be published, says of this move, 'The members met in the morning almost strangers to each other – they spent the evening like brothers, and if they had been all their lives acquainted, and separated rejoicing in the friendships they had formed, and in the expectation of often meeting again.' The Grand Club had got off to an excellent start, and the founding brothers honoured the old Duddingston Club by adopting its rules of play in large part, for these were simple, fair, and of good commonsense. The framing of the constitution was principally the work of the vice-president, Captain James Ogilvie Dalgleish, RN, a Fifer, who for the next thirty years never missed the annual meeting. Like his president, he conceived the constitution first and foremost as a means to one principal objective, which is that of the Royal Club today: 'To unite curlers throughout the world into one Brotherhood of the Rink.' For curling was already spreading abroad, first across the Atlantic to Canada, and then to England and the United States.

Four years after the founding, Queen Victoria and Albert paid their first visit to Scotland. She was only twenty-three and had married Prince Albert just two years earlier. Her notion of a journey to Scotland arose from the recent opening of a railway line. She experimented first on a short local line from Paddington to Windsor. All did not go well, for her Master of Horse, whose function it was to oversee the queen's travel, 'was much put out by this innovation'. When the queen boarded the train, he required her coachman to mount the engine and preside over the driving. The man's scarlet livery was so badly soiled with coal-dust and soot that he quailed at thought of a four hundred miles' expedition into darkest Scotland. He would mount no more engines. But Her Majesty was undeterred. A week or two later, she and the prince steamed north.

They stayed near Perth at the Palace of Scone, whose owner, the earl of Mansfield, was by happy chance president of the Grand Caledonian Curling Club. His club's members suggested that they present Prince Albert with a pair of curling stones, in the hope that he might consent to become the club's first patron. Mansfield agreed, and when the stones arrived at Scone they were seen to be worthy specimens. The masons had made them of fine-grained granite from Ailsa Craig, worked to a mirror-finish, furnished with silver handles, and suitably inscribed.

When Mansfield made the presentation, the young queen was smitten by curiosity. How was the game played? Lord Mansfield rose to the occasion. His palace had an oak-floored ballroom, and he was not a curlers' president for nothing. He had the floor cleared and soon the stones were roaring down the rink. The floor's wax polish assuredly came to grief, but the game was worth the candle. The queen was amused. She and Albert both tried their hands. The queen was taken aback by the great weight of a curling stone. When she tried to throw it she failed, and when told of the length of a real

ANNUAL

OF THE

ROYAL

Grand Caledonian Curling

CLUB,

FOR 1844.

PRINTED FOR
THE ROYAL
GRAND CALEDONIAN CURLING CLUB,
BY THE PERTH PRINTING COMPANY.

Title-page of the 1844 *Annual* with for the first time an engraving of Harvey's *The Curlers*, which still appears on the annual volumes. The word 'Grand' was subsequently dropped from the title of the Club as being superfluous.

rink expressed astonishment that curlers could throw such weights so far. (Albert had not yet presented her with Balmoral, where she would see what weight-throwers could do at Highland Games.)

The result was that in 1843 Prince Albert became patron, and the Grand Club became the Royal Caledonian Curling Club. The patrons have ever since been members of the royal family. Since 1900, they have been the king or queen.

The Royal Club's membership had initially been 28 clubs. Two years later the number had doubled – and continued to rise through the century to 655 by the close. They represented over twenty thousand curlers. The growth in numbers can be ascribed in no small way to a parallel growth in road, rail, and postal services. The new railways had been opening from 1825 onwards. They allowed curlers far more opportunities to meet, play, and confer. Just as Queen Victoria's visit to Scotland had been prompted by rail-travel and would not have been made otherwise, so too with her subjects to some lesser degree. Winter travel especially grew easier as the rail network slowly spread. Of no less importance was the introduction in 1839 of the penny post for all parts of Great Britain, followed immediately by the issue of postage stamps. Until then, postal charges had varied with distance, and senders had to pay cash on posting. Inter-club communication was transformed by that change.

Another strong fertiliser of growth from 1839 was the distribution of the Royal Club's *Annual*. From the start, it strove for national conformity on rules of play, rink length, and stone weights and shapes. It spread the gospel of brotherhood; given that, it argued, members could more readily agree on the few rules needed, while without it no multiplication of rules would ever suffice. The club held tenaciously to that creed and policy, and the years proved it wise. Curling is quite outstanding among the world's sports for the goodwill generated between curlers of all nations – in mountaineering alone is the same fraternity seen. This means no blunting of rivalries, for these give all the stronger respect.

The creation of the Royal Club was well timed for its practical function: to keep curlers at home and abroad in touch with each other. It passed information on the topics of the day and the more interesting subjects in need of discussion, what clubs and provinces were playing where, the names of secretaries and their changes, the new clubs annually forming or affiliating to the Royal Club in Britain and overseas, the results of the matches they played, and the increase in numbers. The *Annual* was thus developing a dual role: uniting the home clubs, and winning acceptance overseas of rules and traditions, thus to make curling an international sport. That it could do this at all was made possible by that intangible 'brotherhood of the rink', an element as real as the rock of Ailsa Craig.

The club's annual meetings in early days, when rules of play were amended or introduced, has been likened to a curlers' parliament. Tactful lobbying could be needed in advance, lords and commons were on equal footing, and the government of the day had to be open-minded, ready to back down if a proposition were not accept-able to the house. Thus, when they required that curlers should use 'foot-irons' (Cairnie's crampit – a strip of sheet-iron, 3 feet 9 inches by 9 inches) on all rinks, such a strong counter-appeal for the hack came from the 'constituencies', that the club had second thoughts and the hack (a foot-length notch, cut longitudinally) was permitted. (The present-day hack in Scotland can be either the 'raised' hack, which is a rubber-covered plate pronged below to fit holes bored in the ice, or else the 'sunken' hack, rubber-lined, as used in some of the indoor rinks and thoughout Canada.) The rule that rinks of eight players be replaced by four, each playing two stones, had to be much delayed, but the change was made after mid-century. Like-wise, the rink diagram was augmented: an obligatory middle line was drawn across the rink to allow for a change in the sweeping rule. The Duddingston rule had allowed the player's party to sweep only from the farther hog-score, but the Ayrshire curlers strongly objected, preferring the earlier rule that allowed sweeping from tee to tee. Therefore the club had to come to a compromise, and in 1852 introduced the middle line from which sweeping might start. The new rule was most valuable. It brought the art of sweeping once again to the fore. It perhaps helped Ayrshire's masters of the twist, who with much brushing could better delay a stone's curl until the last moments. The beneficial effects of vigorous and well-judged sweeping in fetching a stone up the rink had to be seen in all departments of play to be fully appreciated.

Two other important changes were made, the one bound up with the other – rink length and stone weights. The Duddingston rules, which had given a rink of 44 yards, minimum 36, had not mentioned stone-weights at all (the time not seeming ripe). The Royal Club, in the course of its first fifty years, fixed the rink at 46 yards overall,

82

Raith Lake, Fife, c. 1860

Three rinks in play on Stanely Reservoir, Paisley, in about 1880.

giving 42 yards from foot-score to tee (minimum 32 yards for bad conditions), and limited stone weights to fifty pounds maximum. In practice, few stones of such weight were played – the average was 35 to forty pounds. The reason for giving the stone 42 yards of

running length was (according to W. A. Creelman in *Curling Past and Present*) that when a stone of average weight was delivered by the curler of average strength, who gave it the turn that his skip asked, practice had shown that the stone would start its curl close to

Lenzie Loch, early twentieth century

entering the house, if the rink-length were as stated. The house-circle which had varied over the years between a one foot and 6 feet radius, was fixed at 7 feet, with optional inner circles at 2 and 4 feet.

With the formation of the Royal Club and change in rulings, much more attention was being given to the analysis of sole shapes and their performance, and to the craft of making the stones. The lesson had long since been learned that a flat-edged sole collects refuse and sprays up any water, whereas if gently rounded it 'wins its way like a duck'. But what were the determining factors in shape and weight thought to be?

Experiments by John Rennie, one of the leading civil engineers of his age (*ex* Edinburgh), had shown that the amount of friction caused by one body moving along another was determined not by the extent of the moving surface but by the weight of the body. Hence, if stones were equal in weight, even if not in size, the friction brake remained the same; therefore the distance they travelled would depend not on size but on velocity. But if two stones were not equal in weight, the heavier would have this advantage – it would perform better on slushy ice because comparative to weight it would present less surface to air, snow or water. It was thought that on keen ice, weight on a broad bottom helped stability and prevented the stone from being spun off course; and on slushy, a narrower diameter sole would cut more easily down to hard. The consequence was that reversible soles became the order of the day in the 1880s. The preferred running diameters varied from 4 to 7 inches for keen ice, and 2 to $2\frac{1}{2}$ for drug ice. It must be remembered that all this was for outside play. The Royal Club's chaplain, the Reverend John Kerr, advised his flock, and not without reason, that 'Choice of stones is almost as important as the choice of a wife. It must not be done lightly or inadvisably.' On one point at least everyone seemed agreed by the 1890s: the best weight of stone for a good game was around forty pounds.

Before the Royal Club was formed, several of the counties had been meeting at bonspiels with up to forty rinks a side. The club's policy was to encourage bigger and better matches, for these brought together men of like mind and enthusiasm who otherwise would not have the chance to meet and know each other. If a national bonspiel fostered friendships it would serve the best interests of the game.

To further these aims, Ogilvie Dalgleish in 1846 came up with a new proposal. Observing that counties were not always the best units for a curling framework, since their boundaries had no reference to curling opportunity, he urged that the clubs be organized instead in provinces, which would be natural districts, not political. The local curling clubs would thus associate in groups convenient for access to ice, meetings, and matches, as road, rail and local topography provided. This being approved, the affiliated clubs were accorded their districts in 1848, and formed themselves into 16 provinces, each of 6 or more clubs.

The Royal Club, having already conceived the Grand Match or national bonspiel, had hoped that Dalgleish's provinces would run not only their own competitions, in which one province would be drawn against another, but would help to prepare for the Grand Match. The plan turned out to be not a practical ideal. Prolonged frosts were neither sufficiently frequent nor uniform through districts to allow for inter-province matches, and office-bearers were involved in more time-consuming and expensive work than they were able to afford. A much more practical object in the provinces – and one that made their institution most rewarding – was their organization of spiels to find the best club in each district.

County matches continued alongside provincial and parish, played in all for several hundred handsome trophies, cups, medals, and small prizes, offered for competition either by the clubs themselves, or by their many patrons and by the Royal Club. In earlier days, the stake in parish matches had often been bolls of barley and oats, or bags of coal, which the losers bought and distributed to the poor and needy of their districts. Parish spiels continued to be the foundation of Scottish curling to the end of the century and beyond. It appears to have been accepted by all that the best qualities of the game were brought out there. In the end, it was the provincial competitions – not inter-province, but between the teams within each province – that best met the needs of the new century and survived to this day.

The National Bonspiel, now about to be launched in the 1840s, had other values of a different kind.

Every ancient club has to live through recurring cycles of abounding energy, waning life, and exciting renewal. The Royal Club had soared like a rocket off its Waterloo pad. 'The flush of success in their new ventures was upon them, the themes of which they spoke were fresh, and the times in which they lived were prosperous.' Thus wrote John Kerr, sadly reminiscent (maybe in the dogdays), when he felt that the rocket was coming tumbling back to earth. That was after the Jubilee year of 1888. But curlers weather the cycles better than most, for the rink game had taught them to hang on for the upturn.

Great days for curling lay ahead.

Grand Matches

The Grand Matches were inaugurated in one of the great curling winters of the nineteenth century. It came in 1846-47. The lochs froze for three months from December to February. It came as manna from heaven for the sorely tried planners of the Royal Club. They had laboured in vain to set up a match for several counties in 1844, and then a national bonspiel for 1845, when the men north of the Clyde-Forth line would meet the men from the south. The match had been planned for Airthrey Loch, two miles north of Stirling. Thick ice was required, and as usual the frosts failed.

The bearing qualities of ice had since early days been thoroughly investigated by the British Army. The findings had a practical value for curlers. Two inches supported men spaced six feet apart; four inches, a man on horseback; six inches, horse-drawn waggons, or eighty-pounder guns; eight inches, a horse-drawn battery of artillery; ten inches, an army; and fifteen, a railway line. Curlers can play at two inches only if they keep well spaced, and do not build up the house, or sweep in pairs, or cluster the stones anywhere: in short they might practise but not properly curl. Only above two inches are they safe. A bonspiel needs four inches and a Grand Match six. The build-up takes two or three weeks or more according to the degree of cold.

Penicuik, 1847

As soon as the frost of December 1846 was seen to be lasting, the Royal Club acted, and Sir George Clerk of Penicuik gave permission for the use of his loch. The match was called for 15 January. It was agreed to play for three hours from noon, to allow for the distance people had to travel in a short day, and because that time was adequate for a fair test of skills. The match would be decided by totalling the shots scored by each side between the firings of a gun at start and finish.

Penicuik House lay ten miles south of Edinburgh, and nearly two miles from the town of Penicuik and the Caledonian Railway, so the people arrived on horseback, or horse and cart, or by open carriage-and-pair, but most on foot. The day came bright and clear, without snow on the ground. The loch was well sheltered from any wind. Its grassy banks were ringed by well-grown deciduous trees, whose crests gave a high, undulating skyline. The twigs and grass were frosted but the people were not feeling the cold, as shown by their relaxed attitudes in a painting made at the time by Jemima Wedderburn. This painting, and the many others of bonspiels last century, show that any kind of clothing was acceptable on the rink. Curlers 'came as they were', in the daily dress of their station, with surprisingly few visible additions to keep out cold. The city men, and landowners too, turned out in their frock-coats, some even with pin-stripe trousers, and all with silk hats. A few townsmen liked 'stove-pipes' but the counties favoured tall beavers, which like the silk hats had wavy brims. Countrymen wore long tweed jackets and breeches with flat caps and bonnets. The bonnets were the Kilmarnock and blue bonnets, the latter most popular in the Border counties and north of the Highland Line. The kilt was worn by few; clansmen wisely preferred tartan trews. Tartan plaids were thrown over their clothing by men and women of all ranks when they felt a need.

Three hundred curlers arrived for this first national bonspiel. Sixty-eight rinks came from the South, but only twelve from the North. The Grand Match had thus twenty-four rinks, and the remaining forty-four played a match arranged as Midlothian versus the rest. When the signal gun fired at three o'clock, the South had won by 238 to 216. Enjoyment had been huge and news of it spread.

The first Grand Match, Penicuik, 15 January 1847, by Wedderburn.

Grand Match at Linlithgow Loch by Lees

Linlithgow, 1848

Building on the first, the second Grand Match drew nearly seven hundred curlers and five thousand spectators. It was held the following year, 25 January 1848, on Linlithgow Loch. The North had thirty-five rinks, and the South after matching them had a hundred more left over for the side-match.

The arrival of this huge crowd in Linlithgow was watched from an early hour by the Rev. James Taylor, who describes it in *Curling, The Ancient Scottish Game* (1884). All forenoon they poured into the quiet town from all parts of the land. Every train disgorged hundreds, and all forenoon carriages and carts loaded with passengers came rattling through every inlet. Among them were strapping lads from the hills, red-cheeked farmers in big top coats from the south country, spruce Edinburgh men, dressed as if for their board-rooms and banks, the Atholl Highlanders in tartan-banded bonnets, and a host of others, some in riding breeches, or with hose or gaiters or thigh-boots pulled over their trouser-legs. The variety was endless.

A mist had hung over the loch all morning, gradually lifting to reveal a great white expanse from which an inch of snow had been scraped clear on a hundred and fifty green-black rinks. On its south side, the loch was overlooked by the royal palace, which stood on top of a low hill, flanked by trees. Mary Queen of Scots had been born there. Ruined by Hawley's Dragoons after the rising of 1745, its high walls speckled with few and tiny windows looked blank and eyeless. Beyond and behind, low hilly ground swept away into open country, where thin lines of trees marked the fields. The early morning mist had everywhere thickly hoared the trees, shrubs and taller plants. When the sun came out they sparkled as if lit from within. A light fall of dry powder sprinkled the ice: 'Just sufficient,' said Taylor in cheerful mood, 'to give occasional employment to the "sooping" department.'

A thousand curlers had been expected by the Royal Club, but the additional weight of five thousand spectators, who would tend to congregate where play was most interesting, caused them real concern, for the loch was deep. Ropes, ladders, lifebelts and buoys, were scattered across the ice in every direction, under care of the police who were brought in to help. Two guns were fired for the start. The first sent the players on to the ice. When the rinks were found and swept and the players ready, the second gun fired. The effect was dramatic, and heard in Scotland for the first time in its long history: the deep boom of hundreds of stones, their roar swelling and dying away into the distance, followed by receding echoes as if from a discharge of heavy guns.

A celebrated painting of the match was done by Charles Lees, and now hangs at Perth Ice Rink. The foreground scene is a very narrow rink, lined by the social élite, whose head and shoulder portraits are faithfully painted. Despite the handicap of his commission, Lees gives such life to the scene round the house, and to the swaying skaters of the background, and to other incidental figures, that the whole is redeemed. The painting is masterly. By its nature, it cannot catch the essence of curling, or reveal the feature of play at Linlithgow that caught Taylor's eye – 'perfect equality and fraternity'. A still better painting of curling was done in 1834 by Sir George Harvey. That one hangs most worthily in the National Gallery of Scotland (with a second original version in private hands).

The Curlers by Harvey

Lochwinnoch, 1850

The third Grand Match, at Lochwinnoch on 11 January 1850, was on several counts more notable than its predecessors. A blessing in disguise graced the choice of site. Harvey of Castle Semple refused his loch to the Royal Club. He could spare no part of its two-mile length. But a neighbouring curler, McDowall of Garthland, offered instead his Barr Meadow below the south end of the loch. He was able to flood the meadow to a depth of only two or three feet and yet give a sheet of ice a mile long by a quarter-mile broad. This was the first time that a pond had been artificially made for a Grand Match; it was to create a long-lasting precedent. No matter how big the crowd, it was safe.

Lochwinnoch lay fifteen miles west of Glasgow, in the middle of the broad valley between the River Clyde and the port of Ardrossan. The hills of east and west Renfrewshire flanked its either side. They rose from the floor in gentle slopes and tree-belts, which today were bowed under snow. As seen from Barr Meadow, the pond lay cupped between snow-ridges, lifting high westward to Mistylaw and Blacklaw, and swelling eastward over Whittliemuir. Marquee tents were pitched along the shore and the castle of Barr overlooked the scene.

To the chagrin of the Royal Club's workers, snow fell heavily at nine o'clock in the morning, blanketing the clear ice. The early arrivals were put to work. All rinks were restored when the match opened at 12.30 p.m. The clubs North of the Clyde brought in 127 rinks, which, when matched by the South, left twenty rinks for the pre-arranged side-match. Match curlers numbered 1096, but there were more besides, and the spectators were uncountable. This was the greatest bonspiel yet held. Dr Taylor records that it enjoyed the truest and best ice: 'Stones, by the slightest touch – as if by magic – ran any distance, requiring gentle and cautious playing.' He records, also for the first time, that numerous women curlers were present.

The participation of women in a match was a much more important event than a present-day curler might think. Even forty years later, the Rev. John Kerr felt able to write: 'Ladies do not curl – on the ice.' He was wrong. They did. But Kerr would not have called them ladies. He gives a long list of more exemplary ladies, who honoured curling as patronesses – a princess, twenty-four duchesses, marchionesses, and countesses, and two hundred and fifty others of lofty rank. They and all the lesser ladies of the land were welcomed to the game by Kerr as lookers-on, but not to play: 'Like Her Majesty at Scone,' he continued, 'the majority find the curling stone too heavy for their delicate arms.'

Mr Kerr has to be pardoned as a man of his times. They were Victorian times, in which his women were bound more tightly than he – bound too into whalebone corsets pulled as tight as they'd go. Their voluminous petticoats and heavy skirts fell to their toes, and their wide-brimmed hats might have roofed a rink. Such clothing and a lack of male muscle were certainly handicaps, but not prohibitions. Much worse was the psychological barrier still to be overcome. When Scotswomen, for example, revolted against their constrictions and first donned breeches to help them to climb mountains, they were stoned in the streets. (They had to travel to the foot of the hills in skirts, which they then 'stashed' behind boulders.) This common prejudice against women joining in 'manly' sports no more stopped women from curling than from climbing, but it cut their numbers down to the spirited few.

That they were spirited indeed is made plain in the first record of a ladies' bonspiel at Loch Ged in Nithsdale around 1840. Two rinks of Capenoch women met two rinks from Waterside (both near Thornhill). A huge crowd gathered to watch. The sun shone but the heat rose, and soon the players were 'fetlock deep in water'. They set their teeth and carried on: 'the channel-stanes, which female arms are supposed to be unable to cope with, being whirled with all the ease of the distaff.' Next year a match was played in Kirkcudbrightshire, when the married women of Buittle challenged the unmarried. They played twenty a side, and the unmarried won. The Sanquhar Club of Nithsdale records other occasions. It may well be that at this early date women's curling was confined to the southwest counties. Their rinks at Lochwinnoch in 1850 were reported without expression of surprise.

The main feature of 1850 was the huge crowds which the ice had to bear. When dense packs gathered round the most popular rink, the ice became greatly biassed. This had caused anxiety at Linlithgow, but was seen with equanimity at Barr Meadow, except presumably by the players. All went off safely, and when the gun boomed the North had its first win at a Grand Match – a majority of 233 shots.

The scene on this occasion was celebrated not in paint as hitherto but in verse, by Principal Shairp of St Andrew's University.

The Lochwinnoch Bonspiel

Cauld and snell is the weather, ye curlers, come gather!
Scotland summons her best frae the Tweed to the Tay;
It's the North o' the Clyde 'gainst the Southern side,
And Lochwinnoch the tryst for our Bonspiel today.

Ilk parish they've summoned baith landward and borough,
Far and near troop the lads wi' the stanes and the broom;
The ploughs 'o the Loudons stand stiff in the furrow,
And the weavers o' Beith for the loch leave the loom.

The braw shepherd lads they are there in their plaids,
Their hirsels they've left on the Tweedside their lane.
Grey carles frae the moorlands wi' gleg e'e and sure hands,
Braid bonnet o' blue, and the big channel-stane.

And the Loudons three, they foregather in glee,
Wi' tounsfolk frae Ayr, and wi' farmers on Doon,
Out over the Forth come the men of the North,
Frae the far Athole braes, and the palace o' Scone.

Auld Reekie's top sawyers, the lang-headed lawyers,
And crouse Glasgow merchants are loud i' the play;
There are lairds frae the east, there are lords frae the west,
For the peer and the ploughman are marrows today.

See the rinks are a' marshalled, how cheery they mingle,
Blithe callants, stout chiels, auld grey-headed men;
And the roar o' their stanes gars the snowy heights tingle
As they ne'er did before, and may never again.

Some lie at hog score, some o'er the ice roar;
'Here's the tee,' 'There's the winner,' 'Chap and lift him twa yards;'
'Lay a guard,' 'Fill the port,' and now there's nocht for't
But a canny inwick or a rub at the guards.

Gloamin' comes; we maun pairt; but fair fa' ilk kind heart,
Wi' the auld Scottish blood beating warm in his veins;
Curlers! aye we've been leal to our country's weal,
Though our broadswords are besoms, our targes are stanes.

We are sons o' the true hearts that bled wi' the Wallace
And conquered at brave Bannockburn wi' the Bruce;
Thae wild days are gane, but their memories call us,
So we'll stand by langsyne and the guid ancient use.

And we'll hie to the spiel, as our faithers afore us,
Ye sons o' the men whom foe never could tame;
And at nicht round the ingle we'll raise the blithe chorus
To the land we lo'e weel and our auld Scottish game.

Carsebreck, 1853-1935, and after

Two points were now seen to be essential for the success of Grand
Matches; first, that the lochs should be chosen for close access by
railway, thus allowing large attendance, and second, shallow water.
The first point had been appraised immediately after Penicuik; the
second, not officially till after Lochwinnoch. In the summer of 1851,

Sir John Ogilvie moved at the Royal Club's Annual Meeting, 'That the Royal Club should have a piece of ground which could be flooded for the purpose of affording a safe sheet of ice for the Grand Matches.' Sir John had been at Linlithgow, and there been appalled at the prospect of the ice breaking under the weight of six thousand people. And numbers were growing. The Barr Meadow episode had shown how a safe pond could be made given the right site. Ogilvie's motion was approved and a committee formed to search.

The choice fell on Carsebreck in Perthshire. It was a farm in Strathallan, eleven miles north of Stirling, and close beside the Scottish Central Railway. The Royal Club leased from the tenant farmer 63 acres of low ground alongside the Allan Water for £15 per annum, which gave them full use over the four months November to February. The pond was constructed in 1852. Embankments were made, thick moss and peat removed from the clay, and sluices cut. The job was completed that autumn, when the flooded pond gave soundings of six inches at the shallow end to nearly six feet at the west end, where no rinks would be drawn. On 28 November, the first splendid sheet of ice had formed at Carsebreck. The first match was held three months later. Sir John Ogilvie presented to the club a six-pounder cannon, captured by one of his family during Napoleon's siege of Acre in 1799, to be fired at the start and finish. **1853** The first Grand Match at Carsebreck was held on 15 February, after two and a half drenching and dismal winters. The scene is here reconstructed from next day's report in the *Scotsman* newspaper.

The railway companies ran special trains drawing more than twenty carriages, and offering return journeys for single fares; they made a generous allocation of rolling stock; and all this provision fell far short of demand. The trains were crammed beyond capacity. The engines proved unequal to the loads, and the main body of curlers arrived an hour late. At the 'cannon's opening roar' there were 1,432 men on the rinks and a numberless host spectating.

Carsebreck had little of the landscape variety of former sites. In the early morning light it seemed bleak and cheerless. It lay under long snow-slopes bare of trees. On the far side of the strath, the white barrier of the Ochils stretched twenty miles from Forth to Tay. Far westwards, the much higher peaks of Ben Vorlich and Stuc a' Chroin pricked out diamond-white against blue sky. In the brilliant clarity of the forenoon, the scene took life from the sparkle of the vast moor and the ant-like host now spreading over the crescent of ice – a host nearly as big as that of the Jacobite army of 1715, when it moved down this very strath to the battlefield of Sheriffmuir.

The battle today seemed hardly less enthralling, if judged by the eager onset, the boom of artillery, the nervous excitement, the quiet reserve of skips, the shouting, running, kneeling, jumping, the gestures and appeals to heaven, and in short the variety of men of low and high degree, amongst whom the only title to repute was skill at arms. Their number most notably included a rink from Quebec, where curling had now been played for 93 years.

The late start was a real misfortune. It became so warm that many players stripped to their shirt sleeves. Some had been playing on white ice, some on black, but all surfaces became drug. Half the stones thrown were hogs. Then a drizzle began to fall. Some had to shorten their rinks; a few abandoned play in despair as the water deepened. The sensation of the day was caused by Midlothian's Currie rink skipped by Alexander Cunningham: they defeated Lochgelly by 71 shots to 1. Despite which, the North won the Grand Match by 333 shots. They were in better practice after January frosts not shared by the South.

1861 The agonizing decisions that had to be taken by office-bearers and especially by the secretary of the Royal Club, are illustrated by the frost of late December, 1861. The pond was bearing, and the match was called for Hogmanay, but a thaw on the 30th spread half an inch of water over the surface. By nightfall, the water had deepened to a full inch. Commonsense declared 'cancel'. One thousand four hundred curlers should not be brought from the four quarters of Scotland to play on a couple of inches of water, for that is what it could be by morning. Yet the secretary hung on. No Grand Match had been possible over the four years from 1856-59. And 1860 had seen a corresponding drop in numbers. There was a need to maintain the match, he felt. So he spent a sleepless night watching – everything now staked on his 'nose' for a weather-change. At midnight, a slight frost could be detected. At 4 a.m. the frost became effective. By 11 a.m., Carsebreck 'presented as fine a sheet of ice as curlers ever saw even in dreams'.

1873 Twenty-five Grand Matches were played at Carsebreck in the 83 years ending 1935. On 13 February 1873, the day after the match of that year, there appeared in the *Daily Review* an eye-

Carsebreck by Charles Martin Hardie

witness report of the human scene at Carsebreck. When cut in
length, and slightly reworded for the sake of clarity, it epitomises
the Grand Matches of last century:

'Whatever differences of social grade might exist amongst them
were not at all apparent – they were put aside for the day, banished
by that glorious, equalising quality of the game. The sun shone
brightly from a cloudless sky, tempering the asperity of the fresh
northerly breeze. The long slopes of hilly ground in which Carsebreck nestles were scantily clad in snow.

'When the train with the Midlothian contingent of curlers drew up
opposite the loch, it was already a busy scene, which their arrival
heightened. Almost the whole of the cresent-shaped pond was an
unbroken sheet of ice. Far away in the south-western corner there
was indeed a little space of open water, caused probably by springs
rising from the bottom. But the strength of the ice was attested not
only by the large numbers who crowded on to it, but by the fact that
the very edge of the open water could be approached with safety.
The Edinburgh train was one of the last to arrive, and curlers from
north, south, east, and west were now hurrying about, finding out
the rinks assigned to them, marshalling their forces, and describing
the mystic circles of the tee, soon to become such all-absorbing
centres of attraction.

'Curlers were by no means monopolists of the ice. A number of
skaters, scenting from afar such an opportunity of enjoying their
favourite pastime, had accompanied the curlers, and were gliding
over the loch in all directions. Urchins from the scattered farm-
steadings in the neighbourhood, with here and there a rosy-
cheeked lassie, the very personification of health, swelled the

106

number of non-curlers. Those who could not skate devoted themselves to the exhilaration of sliding. Curlers or their satellites continually traversed the ice in all directions, dragging at their heels long trains of curling stones, whose polished surface and bright metal handles glittered in the sunlight. All was bustle – all was apparently confusion; but out of this chaos order was gradually shaped, and when at last the signal gun, perched by the flagstaff on the Kiln Knowe – the hillock which stands so boldly forward in the bend of the loch – was fired to betoken that the hour of noon had arrived, and that business must begin, it was at once clear that the last hour had not been wasted.

'At the same moment play began on more than eighty rinks. On all sides was to be heard the "roar" of the stones, the click of the collisions, and above all the instructions bawled forth by the skips to the players at the opposite end of the rinks. The battle had commenced in good earnest, and now was the time for noting the peculiarities of the different players, and the influence upon them of good and bad fortune.

'At some of the rinks no spectators gathered – the players were left entirely to themselves. But these were the very places where the game could be seen to best advantage. The "operators" on these rinks were pre-eminently men of business, whose hearts were too much on their work to give their tongues time to wag. Silently they played end after end; even the skips communicating their suggestions and commands by signs as much as words. An occasional "Bring her up!" or "Soop her in!" was sufficient to urge the sweepers to the utmost activity. The emphatic planting of the broom on the spot which it was most desirable to reach, or the pointing of it at the stone which it was needful to knock out of the way, conveyed the skip's wishes to the player as effectually as the most detailed instruction.

'Much more excitement and fun, along with equally good play, could be had at the more numerous rinks where the curlers were less subdued in mood. Here you might see a veteran skip, whose town-cut costume of sober grey or black proclaimed him a southerner, bawling to his fellow players, with a vehemence that made his voice hoarse and his face purple, an incessant torrent of hints and directions. "Rub it ca-a-anny," cried one, pointing to a stone which he wished to see raised a little, and giving to the adjective a prolonged intonation, which seemed like a vocal reflection of the precise movement his follower's stone ought to take. "Just dra-aw it to the tee," shouted another, in tones at once loud and insinuating, moving his broom in the line he wished the stone to take. "Hech, mun! that's a thunnering cast ye've gi'en for a draw," he continued, as the stone rattled over the ice at about twice the proper pace. Each skip and each player had his own peculiar style. At one rink a skip might be observed whose excitement found vent in frequent and diligent sweeping of the tee, when he was not engaged in pounding with the flat of his broom the precise spot to which he desired the stone next in order to be played. His rival at the same tee would, on the contrary, perhaps prefer to leave the sweeping to his team, and devote his energies entirely to the task of directing the players. Many and various were the forms in which those directions were given. "Can ye see *this*" (pointing to some particular stone which it was desirable to guard or attack), was a common preliminary inquiry; and when the answer was received, sometimes only after much bawling, it was followed by the instruction, which was almost invariably very shrewd, "I want a guard for this" – "Send her up in a hurry" – "Draw *quiet* for the tee" – "I want this just raised a foot or twa" – "Put her just *there*" (with an emphatic poke of the broom) . . . Then the reception accorded to the stones varied too, most amusingly. "She'll doo it" – "A wee bittie strong" – "Bring her up – *soop, soop*!" – "Let her come – Oh! the bonny wee stane" – "Great shot" – "Oh, ye villain!" were among the cries that rang in all parts of the field of battle.

'As for the players, silence was their portion, save when they had to respond to some query from the skip. Some in delivering the stone stood up a little, as though about to bowl at cricket; others

108

Carsebreck, 1928

stooped low, and scarcely raised the stone from the ice at all. Occasionally you might see an eager player following his stone almost up to the tee, bending his body in the direction in which he desired it to go, as though he could guide it by his will; or he would fall upon hands and knees after delivering it, watching its course in that undignified position, and absolutely unconscious for the moment of everything else in the world.

'As a rule, the North players seemed to be more quiet than their opponents; but there were exceptions, who exhibited true Celtic fire and vehemence. It chanced that at one rink in particular, where much good play was shown, both parties were equally vociferous and the combined attraction of voice and play brought a crowd of spectators throughout the day. The southern skip was a town councillor. He threw himself heart and soul into his work, and well he performed it, both as a skip and player. Some of his instructions were droll. Thus, one of his party having sent up a stone to lie near the tee, our skip announced to his next player, "Play a guard for that – I want a greedy kind o' gaird." He invariably took the most sanguine view of each shot till the stone came up to or passed the tee, and however wide of the mark it might be, he never expressed, nor did his countenance display, any disappointment. He was fortunate in having as second an excellent player, who was also the most demonstrative individual on the ice. Any good shot made on his side elicited a dance of delight, a vehement "hurrah!" or a wave of his broom, while a bad one plunged him for a moment into the depths of despair. *"Do* gi'e it a *soop,* cooncillor," he would cry, in tones of piteous entreaty, if a stone came up too slowly for his taste. "Oh, man! for the love of the game keep a clean tee!" was another; while, after a brilliant inwick shot, he responded to a compliment with the remark, "Did I no' tell you I wis an encyclopaedia."

'At last the signal gun ended play. The best possible testimony to the healthy moral and physical influence of curling is that, during the whole game, the most uniform good temper was displayed, and that only one simple appeal to the umpires was made. Most of the players departed before the final result was announced; and those bound for the north cheered vociferously, apparently labouring under the impression that they had won the day. But, as on some other occasions, the southern players again proved victorious.'

The Carsebreck pond deteriorated over the years. It became congested with weed and the water level was raised to nearly eight

110

feet. By the 1930s its upkeep was becoming too expensive in time and money. The last national bonspiel there was in 1935 – most appropriately the biggest of all. There were 2,576 curlers at the rinks. Thereafter Carsebreck was abandoned. No further Grand Matches were called until after the Second World War of 1939-45.

When the war ended, the frequency of Grand Matches was severely cut by a long sequence of mild winters. Thus far, 34 matches had been played. Three more were successfully called at Loch Leven in 1959, and at Lake of Menteith in 1963 and 1979. Such huge gaps of fourteen and sixteen years had never occurred in previous centuries. The Victorians had felt ill-used with gaps of just three or four years. Since the mid-nineteenth century, the winters had grown milder, not in the sense that annual frosts were absent, but that they were not lasting long enough to give ice for the bigger bonspiels, and in this century rarely even for skating. The game must have suffered danger of death last century, and certain death this century, had the outdoor artificial rink not arrived when it did, to be followed by the indoor rink.

Cairnie's invention of 1827 was adopted gradually, then improved rapidly through the nineteenth century, until every club that could raise the money had an outdoor artificial rink; many had artificial ponds. The difficulty lay not in making the rink or pond, but in maintaining it free of cracks. Concrete and asphalt were much used to get waterproof beds, when a game could be had on a skin of ice usually half an inch to an inch thick, at air temperatures close below freezing point. The revolution they were about to cause – for the transfer of the game from the outdoor to indoor rinks had become inevitable, granted hindsight – could not then be foreseen. 'If we had frost enough,' declared John Kerr in 1890, 'we would condemn all kinds of cement and artificial ponds. They raise the price of curling and destroy the glorious roar of the channel stone.'

Scotland's winter climate had in fact changed. The new rinks were a boon. This was illustrated in the records of the Grand Matches by the huge preponderance of South wins over North – 28 matches to 4 in the period 1847-1914. The reason was that the South had many more artificial rinks (and shallow ponds too) on which the game could be played much more often, with corresponding increase in skills. It's an ill wind that blows no one any good. The warmer wind of the new century blew curlers the tarmac rink. Cheaper and better than concrete, it spread everywhere, so that with less frost than ever before in their history, Scottish curlers had more ice, more play, and a further-evolving game.

Before tracing these Scottish changes into a new era, we must take hold of another strand of change, and twist it together with the first. The new strand was the growing army of curlers abroad. Scottish curlers had been prodigal in giving their skills and ideas to other lands through the nineteenth century. Before long, it would be their turn to receive.

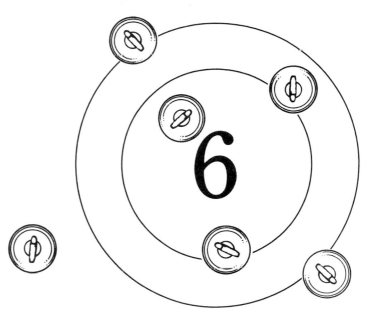

The Game Goes Abroad: 1760-1981

England

The Border between Scotland and England is no unreal line on the maps. It marks, sometimes more effectively than the broad Atlantic, a line of social cleavage. Thus curling was introduced by the Scots to Canada in 1760, fifteen years before it was played in England. Likewise, the first club to be formed beyond Scotland was in 1807 at Montreal; the first in England, at Leeds in 1820. The county of Dumfries had fostered curling for centuries; it lay along the divide between the two nations; yet not until around 1775 did the game cross the Border to Cumberland.

The first indication of play in England was when some old curling stones were discovered in Cumberland in the river Line, just two or three miles across the border from Gretna. That was in 1836, and only then was it found that the rector of the Cumberland parish had been curling with his friends some fifty years earlier. There is no record of play until 1811, when a few Scots curled on New River, a canal in north London, attracting so large a crowd (probably of their own countrymen) that the ice was in danger of breaking. They were obliged to give up the game.

Curling at Manchester, 1877

Scotsmen were meanwhile becoming more numerous and influential in the north of England. In 1820, they formed the first curling club at Leeds, another at Liverpool in 1839, and so by a slow spread, confined to the northern counties, 37 clubs were playing by 1914. The first to join the Royal Club was Liverpool, and the others followed. The Royal Club gave much encouragement and the first international contest was called in 1895 at Talkin Tarn, and the next two at Lochmaben. From 1907 it became an annual event, although not truly international in its early years, for most of England's players were Scots.

Indoor rinks alone made such annual events possible. England's most important contribution to nineteenth century curling was the invention of a means for making artificial ice. The first rink with such ice was built in London in 1842. It measured only seventy feet by fifty feet, and therefore could be used only by skaters. Thirty years later a new ice-making process was invented by Professor Gamgee. In 1877, a rink using his method was opened at Manchester, and the world's first curling match on artificial ice was played there in March. The owning company promptly failed, but a new rink opened in 1879 at Southport in Lancashire. That same year, six English clubs held a competition, which became a six-monthly tournament for the Holden Challenge Cup (presented by Edward Holden). From the start, Scottish clubs came south to compete, until the rink company failed in 1890. The cause of failure, ironically, was the sufficiency of outdoor ice, which curlers preferred. The Southport rink had cost £30,000 to build, and the consequent charge to curlers banned play to the working class. There could be no Tam Pates on the indoor rinks (Tam had been a tinker). Few Scots could abide social barriers on the rinks, nor at that time did they like playing indoors. By the turn of the century, outdoor ice had again failed them. The day of the indoor rink had come. But not for England. Four rinks successively closed, the last at Richmond, and now there are none. England's two hundred curlers are obliged to travel to Scotland and Switzerland.

Canada

On the fall of Quebec in 1759, and the death of General Wolfe, Brigadier James Murray took command of the city. One of his regiments was the 78th Highlanders, known as Fraser's Regiment. It had been raised in Inverness-shire by Simon Fraser, Lord Lovat, and commanded by him in the assault on the citadel. He was still a young man and maybe a curler himself, for his men had leisure to play in 1760, and when they could find no suitable stones they were allowed to melt down cannon balls – which they could certainly not have done without permission. They curled on the St Charles River.

The incident was an isolated one, without direct consequence for Canadian curling, unless as a precedent for the use of iron in place of stone, or as the first example of a general rule, that wherever

Scotsmen settled they curled. Canada's first civilian curling would almost certainly start in the eighteenth century, but the earliest reports in the Canadian press are for 1805 at Beauport, near Quebec, and in the town itself at an artificial rink made in 1808 on one of the wharves – the river ice being too rough. Similar games were clearly occurring elsewhere, for Canada's first club was founded in 1807 at Montreal. Named the Royal Montreal Curling Club, its members played on the St Lawrence and tried to keep up the old Scottish traditions – they dined on salt beef and greens and met every fortnight to that good end. Quebec Province had no good rock, so they used irons of 45 lb to 65 lb, at first roughly shaped with high sides. These were the common property of the club.

A second club was formed at Quebec City in 1821. Here too cast-iron stones were used. A Kilmarnock curler in Quebec reported to James Cairnie the words of a French-Canadian farmer when he saw the game for the first time:

'J'ai vu aujourdhui une bande d'Ecossais qui jetaient des grandes boules de fer, faites commes des bombes, sur la glace; après quoi, ils criaient *soupe, soupe*; ensuite, ils riaient, comme des foux; je crois bien qu'ils sont vraiment foux.'

Early Canadian 'iron' of a type still used into the twentieth century.
This one was brought back to Scotland by a member of the 1902 touring team.

'Today I saw a band of Scotsmen who were throwing big iron balls like bombs on the ice; after which they cried "soop, soop", and then laughed like mad; I truly think they *are* mad.'

The iron stones were made by sending a wooden model to the forges at Trois Rivières for casting. Trois Rivières lay halfway between Montreal and Quebec, and here it was that Canada's first curling match was played between the two clubs in 1835. Each team required two days to cover the eighty miles to the site, for the tracks were bad and snow-falls heavy.

Farther west, in Ontario, conditions were still more difficult, communications slower, and population sparser. Curling there received a powerful reinforcement after Napoleon's defeat at Waterloo in 1815. The British government at once relaxed control of emigration, a policy complemented by the Highland Clearances. Approximately forty thousand people emigrated to Ontario alone during the seven years 1816-23. Most were Scots. In 1824, the Scottish novelist, John Galt, formed the Canada Land Company, which acquired land in Ontario to promote Scottish colonization. He founded the town of Guelph, the town of Galt was named after him, and Scottish families poured in. Ontario's first curling club had already been formed at Kingston in 1820. Immigrants from Dumfries and Lanark started curling at Toronto around 1825, and many of them happened to be stone masons. They made their stones from 'granites' and whinstones found in the fields, which they were clearing for cultivation. In 1837, they formed the Toronto Curling Club. Others had already been forming all around. Some took stones from the rivers, but up in the bush country they used blocks sawed from beech and maple trunks. These were satisfactory when weighted with iron bands. The spurs and handicaps to curling were not unlike those of Scotland in the early eighteenth century – no roads, slow travel, small scattered communities living in cold, ill-lit, uncomfortable houses, difficult communications, and play between rinks casually formed. When Toronto played their bi-annual match with the Hamilton Thistles, the visiting team had to allow three days for the game although the towns lay only 55 miles apart. Travelling in sleighs and wagons loaded with stones, besoms, and shovels, the team would spend a full day on the road each way, and half the match-day shovelling snow off the rinks.

As soon as news reached Canada that the Grand Caledonian Club had been founded, the Royal Montreal and Quebec Curling Clubs applied for membership as the Quebec Association. In 1843 they were renamed the Canadian Branch of the Royal Caledonian Curling Club. For thirty years they gave Canada its governing body with headquarters in Montreal. Numerous other clubs were now forming and joining, but few came in from Ontario, for distances were too great, and Quebec's use of irons was a barrier, especially after mid-century when stones imported from Scotland had become plentiful.

The centre of Ontario's curling was Toronto. More rapid development ensued from 1850 with the opening of the Grand Trunk Railway from Montreal to Toronto, and thence to north and west Ontario. Toronto in 1859 was thus able to sponsor the first big bonspiel, between the East and West clubs of the province, on the ice of Toronto Bay. Each side fielded 21 rinks. Early matches between Toronto and Montreal did not, however, bring their two provinces closer. Quebec still insisted on irons. As a compromise, they matched two rinks a side, one using granites, the other irons, with the unhappy result that each always won with its own 'stones'.

The Ontario clubs had no representatives on the Canadian Branch for shaping rules or policy, yet had thrice Quebec's number of clubs. Therefore they united in 1874 and joined the Royal Caledonian Club as the Branch of the Province of Ontario (with the governor general, Lord Dufferin, as patron). The move established a precedent. Ontario henceforth encouraged the western provinces, which initially drew much of their curling strength by immigration from Ontario, to form their independent curling associations and to affiliate directly with the Royal Caledonian.

In the Maritime Provinces, curling spread slowly, hampered as elsewhere by the war with the United States in 1812-14. The first two clubs were in Nova Scotia – at Halifax in 1824, and in Pictou in 1829 when coal-miners from Scotland had the good sense to bring their stones with them. In Newfoundland, another group of Scots formed a club at St John in 1843. In New Brunswick, the impetus to start curling came not from curling immigrants but from an article in the *Glasgow Herald,* which described the Grand Match at Carsebreck in 1853. The local readers took the bait, imported stones, and having once tried the game, were hooked. Their club was formed in 1854. The Royal Caledonian Club helped the Maritime Provinces and all others by giving medals for competition, and much practical advice.

118

Having seeded curling all through the eastern provinces, the Scots (or their second generation) then moved out to the central provinces and on to the west. The very first settlers in Manitoba in 1812 were curlers. They made stones from oak blocks. Seventy years later, the Ontario Branch reported: 'The large emigrations from our Province to the new Province of Manitoba has thinned the ranks of many of our curling clubs; but the emigrants are everywhere carrying with them the love of the game.' And so indeed they were, aided now by the long dry winters of the Prairie Provinces, and by the opening in 1885 of the Canadian Pacific Railway. Just as Toronto had supplanted Montreal as the centre of curling influence, so now Winnipeg ousted Toronto. The clubs of Manitoba multiplied until their numbers exceeded those of Quebec and Ontario together. In 1888 they founded a Manitoba Branch of the Royal Caledonian. The Winnipeg bonspiel of that year had 62 rinks, and the Winnipeg Curling Club (formed in 1876 with an indoor rink – but not with artificial ice) drew curlers from all parts of Canada and the U.S.A.

Saskatchewan Province had curling from the 1880s in widely scattered communities. Numerous small clubs formed within short distances, so that farmers might not have too far to travel. To get protection from wind-driven snow, many of them built thatched wooden huts on top of the natural ice. Numbers grew until Saskatchewan had more curlers than any other province. The early clubs in Saskatchewan, Alberta, and British Columbia were all affiliated with the Manitoba Branch, which encouraged growth while persuading them to form their own provincial associations, and this they all did between 1904 and 1906.

During this century of club growth, curling had been moving indoors. A temperature of 20° below zero Fahrenheit (minus 29°C.) is normal in winter across Canada. To win relief from this intense cold, to protect the rinks from heavy snowfalls, and to enjoy nighttime play, the bigger clubs had begun to build covered rinks from the 1840s onwards: at Montreal in 1847, Toronto in 1859, at Hamilton in 1860, at Ottawa in 1868, at Winnipeg in 1876, and the first palatial rink at Toronto in 1877. The smaller clubs had been slow to build, by reason of cost. But club memberships had so increased by the end of the century, the advent of railways had allowed such frequent bonspiels, that press publicity followed, advertisers were interested, and the captains of industry presented

Bonspiel on Granite Rink, Toronto 1884

medals, prizes, trophies, entailing keener competitions, bigger matches, more publicity, and recruits to the game. On the bandwagon came money. By 1900, all Canadian curling was under cover. The smaller towns built their sheds in wood, the larger in brick, usually with space for four to six rinks.

The method of ice-making had a profound influence on the game, for although it was natural ice, depending on air temperature, it was still made by man's craft. The floor was first made by draining the top soil, and covering that with six inches of well-compacted sand. At some rinks, ten-inch joists were laid across cedar sleepers, and the spaces between packed with ashes; on top of which a tongued and grooved floor was laid in white lead and the wood oiled. Ventilators at the floor and roof admitted cold air and let warm escape.

The ice was made by spraying the floor with successive thin coats until the sheet was watertight. The ice was then given several successive floodings, each of small depth, to allow the water to

120

reach its natural level before freezing, yet to cut the danger of leakage through the first ice-skin. It was then a level sheet an inch thick, some parts glassy, others not if air currents had played on it. The finishing touch had now to be given. This was called pebbling. Hot water close to boiling point was sprinkled on from a pot with a rose. The hot water before freezing melted a seat for itself in the ice-sheet, and so would not scale off under the curling stones' friction. The sprinkler holes were minute and spaced one inch apart in a single row three feet long. The water was thus applied rapidly in straight lines, either at right-angles to form squares or diagonally to form diamonds. (A much finer pebble was later produced by spraying.) This 'pebbled' ice gave the stones, whether of rock or iron, a uniform grip over the length of the rink. It was daily refreshed, for these rinks were in daily use for four to five months of the year, and especially at night, when they were lit by electricity.

The improved ice was matched by improved stones. Although many curlers imported Scottish stones, most settlers made their own stones on the Scottish model. In 1879, J.S. Turner of Toronto, after long experiment with numerous stones and forms of running sole, felt that he had achieved a near perfect stone for all ice conditions. His ideas were applied by the Scottish stone-maker, Andrew Kay of Mauchline in Ayrshire. He machine-tooled the stones to Russell's specification, which he improved upon with technical refinements of his own. This joint product was designed for outdoor rinks, and was soon found to be far superior to those hitherto in use. They were made with keen and dull bottoms. The keen side was slightly concave with an arris (or rim) $^3/_8''$ broad; the dull side, concave to a depth of $^1/_4''$, with a very narrow, rounded arris. The diameter of the cups was 5 to 5$^1/_2''$, the wider giving more borrowing power from its greater resistance. The diameters were so proportioned that the stone had the same borrow when played with the keen bottom on drug ice as it had with the dull bottom on keen ice. The stones were in high demand through North America by the 1890s. When indoor rinks and pebbled ice became general, the stones were given uniform running surfaces with a 5" diameter on both sides. They could be turned over at intervals to give equal wear.

On the indoor rinks, hacks replaced crampits. The crampit on outdoor ice imposed on the player a stationary foot-position. He bent at the waist and knees, but his feet remained in a fixed-stride

The first Scottish team to visit Canada and the United States, 1902

attitude, left foot forward. The Canadians preferred the hack for indoor ice. It completely changed their 'shooting technique'. The hack now gave the toe-grip for the right foot, and changed the angle of delivery. At first the player only bent more at the knees; then he began to move forward a little as the stone was delivered; and finally he swung his left leg forward on delivery, thrusting with his right and sliding on his left toward the target while his straight right arm went forward on the vital follow-through.

The development of the slide, and its accompaniment, the hard-thrown running shot, which led to the 'take-out' game, was principally the work of Canada's leading curler in the 1890s, Bob Dunbar of Winnipeg. He changed the strategy of play, if at first only locally. Canadian curlers had thus far favoured the draw game, in which stones were built up in the house. They had developed the twist to a higher degree of skill than Scotland's players had imagined possible, and accompanied that with brush work of military precision. In Manitoba, Dunbar practised his slide and running shot and follow-through for hour after hour, until he achieved a perfect balance and

Key to the Scottish team, 1902

1. W. Stirling, Galashiels.
2. W. Hamilton, Douglas.
3. J. B. Fergusson of Balgarth, Ayr and Alloway.
4. D. Provan, Craiglockhart.
5. H. Ballantyne, Peebles.
6. R. Bramwell, Upper Nithsdale.
7. J. M'Gregor, Camperdown.
8. H. Prain, Castle Huntly.
9. Dr. Kirk, Bathgate.
10. D. Murray, Kelvindock.
11. D. Bentley Murray, Airthrey Castle.
12. M. Sanderson, Duddingston.
13. T. Simpson of Mawcarse, Orwell.
14. T. Macmillan of Glencrosh, Glencairn.
15. J. Scott Davidson of Cairnie, Hercules.
16. A. T. Simpson, Melrose.
17. R. Johnston, Upper Annandale.
18. W. Henderson, Kinnochtry.
19. A. E. Campbell, Gourock.
20. Rev. John Kerr, Dirleton, (Captain).
21. A. Davidson Smith, Secretary R.C.C.C., Whittingehame.
22. Major Bertram of Kersewell, Medwin.
23. A. Smith, Stenhouse and Carron.
24. E. Gibson, Biggar.
25. G. Deans Ritchie, Broughton United.
26. R. Cousin, Merchiston.
27. D. R. Gordon, Bathgate.
28. R. Husband, Dunfermline.

rhythmic swing, and a slide that took him several feet out of the hack. His rink began to defeat all others of the draw school. His deadly running shots knocked his opponents' stones out of the house. His team refined its shooting to such an art that the Winnipeg Club in 1899 considered banning the slide-delivery, which was not in accord with the current interpretation of the rules. They decided to leave well alone. Younger curlers watched him, imitated him, and tried to improve on his technique. Before the outbreak of war in 1914, Frank Cassidy achieved a nine foot slide in which he threw his whole body towards the target. This was surpassed by Gordon Hudson, who practised a follow through slide on the side of his left foot. This took him 18 feet to the front of the rings before he released the handle.

The heightened skills, the better stones, the pebbled ice, the changes in techniques, came as a revelation to the first Scottish team to visit Canada and the United States in 1902. Several times since 1858, Canadian curlers had been asking the Royal Club to

send out a touring team. At last, in December 1902, they sent out six rinks under the captaincy of the Rev. John Kerr. The Scots started play on the east coast at Halifax in Nova Scotia, and progressed westward playing almost daily through the provinces of Quebec, Ontario, and Manitoba. In mid-February, they moved south from Winnipeg to the State of Minnesota, and played through the states south of the Great Lakes to New York. In all, they played 99 set games of which they won 47, lost 49, and tied three. It was a most creditable performance, especially when they frequently kept late hours, while enjoying unbounded hospitality – and while travelling 5,000 miles (train speeds were only 20 mph) always to meet fresh teams at the journey's end. Their game at first suffered in other ways. The new stones they had brought out had been cut too sharp at the edge of the arris, and 'sent up a spray like a peacock's tail'. The stones became warmed up in travel, for the trains were heated to 70° F. Hence when the stones were played they tended to settle down half-way up the rink, or even to embed themselves, until the Scots learned that stones had to be left standing on ice a full twelve hours before play. Not one of the Scots had played before on a covered rink, and few were accustomed to the hack.

John Kerr published a full report on return to Scotland. The lessons learned on his tour had a powerful effect on the evolution of Scottish play in years to come. A few observations by team members are best told in their own words.

Artist's impression of the covered rink at Winnipeg

124

At Winnipeg, where the Scots played in a bonspiel of 185 matches, five Scottish rinks were pitted against five selected rinks from Canada and the U.S.A. The North Americans won. Kerr reported: 'Play all round was superb, the scientific accuracy of many of the shots, owing to the evenness and hardness of the ice, being such as one can never expect to see in the home country. Many of the players were young men in their teens; in fact, very few veterans were to be seen, the lissomeness of youth being almost a necessity for the system of sweeping which is followed on Canadian rinks . . . The number of prizes and value of the spoil at the Winnipeg Bonspiel seemed to bring out a far more desperate and striking kind of play than we had ever witnessed in our former matches with the clubs in the Dominion.'

His rink members enlarged on these subjects, which I here abbreviate:

Bertram: 'There are two great distinctions between their game and ours: first the splendid way in which they sweep; second, the amount of handle they use, effective partly owing to the beading on their ice, and also to their hack. There is not the slightest doubt that the hack is superior to the crampit. We should abandon the crampit.'

Bramwell: 'I would strongly advise any of you who are investing in new stones to get them with the genuine Canadian bottom on the dull side. If there is any handle to be got they will take it. (Of our own stones, no two pair of them seemed to run alike) . . . Their style of delivery is different. They don't lift the stone so high, but slide away forward with it . . . they keep a better line than we do, and play more of a drawing game – stones are of little account short of the rings – long guards are no use, simply stones wasted . . . they sweep crossways and make the brushes go so fast that they create a vacuum in front of the stone – so they say – and there must be some truth in it, for it was marvellous how far the stones would travel when you thought they were just stopping . . . If the stone were narrow, they would sweep right away; and if wide, they would delay as long as possible till they got it coming right, then they would bring it away. You can see therefore what an important part sweeping takes in the game, and how much easier for the skip with a rink of stones all running alike.'

Campbell: 'Until Winnipeg, play was on the drawing system, with not much striking. At Winnipeg, my experience was one rarely met at home – persistent striking . . . We met there a different class of

players, men who had come for the express purpose of winning prizes, and not so much to meet and play with the Scotsmen . . . We found first and second players to be young and supple, and besides being excellent curlers rarely missing the carrying through process, they were very demons with the broom. This is an art our best sweepers have yet to learn – a great factor in winning. The main distinction between our game and theirs is their giving every stone a turn of the handle, whereas we use it for the most part to counteract a bias on the ice.'

McGregor: 'Canadians are really the best curlers in the world, owing to the enormous amount of practice.'

Simpson: 'To be a successful curler in Canada, one must be a complete master of the out and in turns; the shots that can be taken by one who can work the handle require to be seen to be believed . . . Canadians are far ahead in the art of sweeping or "polishing" the ice . . . The game of curling in Scotland can never be brought to such a state of perfection as is found in Canada until rinks under cover become more general.'

The team had other pointed comments to make. John Bramwell observed that, 'Here (Scotland) curling is a rural game; out there it is essentially a town one. The strongest clubs are found in the large cities. The playing is all done in the evenings.' Lawton added: 'Many of our young men who would be curlers cannot, as all play is during the day; while in Canada it is mostly at night in electric light.' Bertram added this qualification: 'The labouring class, amongst whom are some of the best curlers at home, could not curl in Canada owing to the expense not only of the rink but also of the clubhouse.' A Canadian comment in mitigation was that, 'The levelling process is not just in the social scale. Different politics, religious beliefs, degrees of learning, age, and all else that isolates a man from his fellows, are forgotten.' John Kerr concluded that curling in Canada could be enjoyed with a fulness unknown at home. He had certain reservations. Winnipeg was to curling what St Andrews was to golf in Scotland, 'the hearth of the game in the Dominion', but 'Newspapers all issue glaring headlines . . . competitions, cups, and prizes are valuable . . . enterprising firms by way of advertising provide the numerous trophies . . . but this is "no oor ain game". Somehow it lacked the poetry, the romance, the exhilaration, the excitement of our parish bonspiels at home. They are all very well in their own way, these covered rinks, these palatial premises, these

126

retiring rooms with "a' the comforts o' the Sautmarket", but one crowded hour of glorious play on a hillside loch, with a few vivers (food) on the bank, is worth an age of curling in a covered court.'

Every Scottish curler could share the feelings of the Rev. John Kerr, but the sad fact remained that Scotland's winter climate had changed. There was no longer frost for deep water curling except on most rare occasion; frequency of play depended now on indoor rinks. If the Scots were ever again to meet Canada on such near equality of skill as in 1903, the game in Scotland had to move indoors. Every lesson of the tour had to be applied.

The United States

The Canadian saying, that wherever the Scots settled, there curling began, applied equally to the United States, if less markedly. There is no written evidence of curling before 1832, but since several hundred Scottish communities were scattered through the colony before the War of Independence (1775-83), it would seem virtually certain that informal curling had begun long before record of the first club. The record came from an improbable place, Orchard Lake in the wilds of Michigan. A group of Scottish farmers were migrating by boat through Lake St Clair, heading for Chicago, when they were wrecked on the shore. They liked the site and settled. The winter offered excellent curling, so they met at the house of Dr Robert Burns on 2 January 1832 and formed a club. They sawed blocks from hickory trees, shaped them, and played their first game a few days later.

Wisconsin, c. 1850. Wooden blocks are used as curling stones.

There is record of curling in New York in the 1830s, without any club, hence the New England club of Boston came second in the field around 1839, and Milwaukee third. Curling on the Milwaukee River had begun with wooden blocks in 1843, and the club came two years later. Several other clubs in Wisconsin sprang up in 1850. One of them, at Dekorra, enjoyed an unorthodox birth. It started at the close of a wild Hogmanay party, when the men took to the frozen mill pond at 1 a.m. – using as stones their wives' flat-irons. The game was adjourned at 2.30 a.m. with a challenge for that same afternoon, by which time pairs of blocks had been cut from hickory trees. Some clubs had real stones from the start, like Chicago in 1854, where rocks were picked from the shores of Lake Michigan. The game and the formation of clubs now spread faster with aid from a growing network of railways between the north-east and north-west states.

The time had become ripe for a national club. In 1867, twelve clubs joined together as the Grand National Curling Club of America. It did not at first affiliate with the Royal Club, but used its rules. The first president was David Bell of Dumfries and Buffalo, and their first patron, Robert Gordon, who in 1869 presented the Gordon Rink Medal, for which competitions are still held.

The early members of the Grand National were nearly all from the eastern states. As soon as the western states were settled, more clubs formed and joined, including three Canadian clubs, for the international boundary was no bar to brother Scots. (When ice was poor in the States, the Gordon Rink Medal was played off in Toronto.) Alexander Dalrymple in 1870 presented two Dalrymple Medals for competition, one in each of the east and west regions, between players hailing from the North and South of Scotland as determined by the Forth and Clyde line. Competitions proliferated over the years. The first international bonspiel had been held even before the birth of the Grand National. It took place on Lake Erie in 1865, at Black Rock near Buffalo. Twenty-three rinks turned out for each side, and thousands were present on the ice to watch. It made a lively scene, with flags flying, skaters dashing, and the crowd cheering. Canada won. Robert Gordon later presented his International Medal for this match, which became an annual event from 1888 (except during the World Wars).

In 1880s were years of rapid growth, and the spread of covered rinks. The Grand National Club then chose to divide. Fourteen clubs in the states north and west of the State of Ohio broke away to form the North-western Curling Association. The distances between east and west had been found too great for regular curling and business meetings, and the western clubs were now sufficiently numerous to be self supporting. Both national associations were strong at the close of the century, when the Grand National had 25 clubs, and the North-west 17. The members were now importing granite stones, building rinks, and competing in numerous matches from local to international level. It was then, when the future seemed most bright, that calamity struck.

Twenty years of warm winters, accompanied by war and followed by economic depression, caused eastern curling to die away. It was saved only by a gradual introduction of refrigerated rinks in the 1920s and 1930s. The North-western Association expired. But individual clubs, diminished in number, survived. When better times returned after the Second World War, numbers again grew, curling extended for the first time across the whole country, and the United States Men's Curling Association, founded in 1958, became the governing body. (In 1976 it dropped the word 'Men's'.)

The Rest of the World

It is not a part of my purpose to give a history of curling in all the twenty countries that play it, and the five others that have briefly tried it; but a quick summary of the way it was introduced to and found footing in other lands has its place in the main theme: the development of the game and its evolution to new forms.

1839. Ireland

The Irish winter climate was too mild for any early introduction of curling. When transplanted, it failed to flourish. John Cairnie in 1839, after inventing his artificial rink, persuaded his sailing friend, James Boomer, to make a pond at Belfast. Boomer formed a club and played until his death in 1846. Curling at Belfast, after its lapse, was revived by a small Scottish party, and two other clubs were formed in the hard winter of 1878-9. By the end of the century, all curling had disappeared.

1846. Sweden

Curling was introduced to south-west Sweden, at Uddevalla, by W. A. Macfie of Greenock in 1846. Six years later he founded a club, named the Bohuslanka. At this time, only members of the aristocracy curled, and not until the Stockholm club was founded in 1901 did the game spread. After a visit by Scottish players to Stockholm in 1913, curling began at the popular mountain resort of Are. More clubs formed and joined in the Swedish Curling Association of 1916. Five years after the war, a Swedish team toured Scotland. Nearly forty years of quiet progress ensued, then came an extraordinary upsurge of enthusiasm in the 1960s – this despite the fact that most play was out of doors with a short season of three months' ice in the south. The movement followed the Swedes' adoption of the Canadian style of play; as in North America, it attracted the notice of the young. They entered the world championship in 1962, and thereafter devoted themselves to mastering the slide delivery and take-out game. Hakan Sundström, the Swedish curler, attributes much of their success to coaching by the Canadian Bob Woods, who had settled in Stockholm. They had become competitive curlers. Within five years they were able to reach the world final at Perth (won by Scotland). In compensation, they won back the Swedish Cup (offered for international competition), which Scotland had held since 1965. During that decade, their numbers quadrupled to nearly five thousand. A big indoor curling rink was built in Stockholm, which helped their game further, until in 1973 and 1977, they twice won the world championship. Their numbers have since risen to 5,500 using nearly twenty indoor rinks; and the game is still played out of doors in the north. There is every sign that Sweden, of all European countries, is the one where curling has the greatest potential for growth and development.

1873. New Zealand

Immigrant miners and shepherds from Scotland, many of whom brought their stones with them, introduced curling to South Island in the nineteenth century. They had played for some years before the first club was formed at Dunedin in 1873 – by a Mauchline curler, Thomas Callender. Dunedin was too low. It could count on only a week's ice each year, so a second club was founded that same year at Mount Ida, which at 2,000 feet offered six weeks of good ice. The clubs grew in number until in 1886 seven formed a province under the Royal Caledonian Club. All curling has continued on natural ice to the present day, when four hundred curlers from 26 clubs are competing in bonspiels. All but two clubs are based on the high ground of central Otago.

1873. Russia

A small club was formed in Moscow in 1873 by a Scot named William Hopper. In 1879, Lord Dufferin, who had newly come from Canada to take post as British ambassador, tried to establish a rink at St Petersburg, but failed. Curling at Moscow, which had lasted forty-odd years, ended on the outbreak of war in 1914. It has not been reintroduced.

1880. Switzerland

In 1879, a Scottish curler presented four pairs of stones and a Royal Club rule-book to Johannes Badrutt, the proprietor of St Moritz Kulm Hotel in the Engadine. The gift inspired Badrutt to have yet another four pairs made from local stone, and next winter, on 22 December 1880, Switzerland's first curling match was played at St Moritz at 6,090 feet. There was no further growth at first. Winter sports resorts were few – hotels (even at Wengen) stayed closed

Switzerland in the 1920s

Curling in Switzerland at the rink at Mürren as it is today, where
the game was introduced by British guests in 1910.

from October to June. The weather was ideal for winter sports in
general, and for curling in particular. On the lakes of the high Alps,
thick ice could be expected from December to the end of February,
and with it, blue sky and sun. When the more leisured curlers of
Scotland and England had discovered Switzerland, the hotels

responded. In 1894, the first curling club opened its doors to visitors at St Moritz. Its members immediately affiliated with the Royal Club. Other resorts were opening, and after initial hesitations took up this new game of curling. They found its popularity growing so fast (in the wake of other sports) that by 1914 none of any size or repute was without a rink. Rinks with few exceptions were made, owned, and maintained by the hotels. They often made their rinks on hard tennis courts. The first fall of snow was trodden down, flooded and re-flooded, until the snow had ceased to absorb water, then by successive flooding and spraying a good rink was formed.

Play throughout Switzerland was with Ailsa stones. Their concave bottoms were of four-inch diameter on the keen side, five-inch on the dull, and were usually played on the dull side, for the rink conditions were near perfect. The excellent ice, the mountainous backgrounds, the wooded foregrounds, the reliable sun and good food and comfort, brought an annual inrush of visitors, even when play was for the moneyed elect. In 1898, N. Lane Jackson presented the Jackson Cup for the championship of Switzerland. In 1905, Sir Henry Lunn presented a challenge cup for the Swiss International Bonspiel. Curling spread all over the Swiss Alps to at least 24 resorts.

By the time of the Second World War, the Swiss themselves, not their foreign visitors, had become the moving spirits of the game. In 1942, 16 clubs formed the Swiss Curling Association, who one year later established the first national championship match. When curling sprang into popularity in the 1950s, the indoor rinks extended even to the mountain resorts. From 1964 onwards, artificial ice rinks were built in the valleys at Berne, Basle, Lausanne, Neuchatel, and Zurich. Switzerland today has seven thousand curlers in more than two hundred clubs; and her rinks have twice won the world championship, in 1975 and 1981.

1880. Norway

The earliest record of curling in Norway was the affiliation to the Royal Club in 1882 of the Elverhae club, which had been formed in southern Norway in 1880-81. At that time, it had a close association with members of the Angus club of Evenie Water. Curling did not begin to spread until 1954, after a Scottish rink's visit to Oppdal, where a club was promptly formed, followed by another at Oslo. The Nordic Bonspiel, between Norway and Sweden, began in 1958.

135

The country now has over a thousand curlers in 26 clubs. Like the Swedes, they play both indoor and outdoor. With the help of Canadian coaching, Norway in recent years has greatly increased her international curling status. Kristian Soerum's rink won the world championship in 1979, and was runner-up in 1978 and 1980.

1890. China

A club was formed at Tientsin in 1890 and lasted nearly fifty years. It vanished in 1939 on the outbreak of war.

Since Switzerland was Europe's playground, curling there led to the game's introduction to other nations of the continent, to which a Scottish game would not otherwise have reached. Given the Swiss example, they often called on the Royal Club or its members to give aid at the start. The countries to which curling thus spread in the twentieth century were (with the one exception of Australia, here included to keep the chronological order):–

1912. Austria

Kitzbuhel had two years' curling to 1914. Play resumed there when Scottish curlers brought it back in 1955. Two clubs were formed, since which five others have grown in the Tyrol and Vienna. Austria now has 125 curlers.

1912. Italy

Curling began at Cortina at 5,000 feet in the Dolomites only to end abruptly in 1914. It resumed there in 1957. The Italian Curling Association now has five clubs.

c 1920. France

Curling began early in the century at a few resorts in the Haute Savoie. When the Olympic Winter Games of 1924 were held there, at Chamonix, national curling matches received encouragement; that brought publicity and a growth of fifty clubs. The governing body since 1941 is the curling committee of the French Federation of Ice Sports.

1936. Australia

Three Scots introduced curling to the ice rink at Melbourne in 1936.

The game died when war broke out in 1939, and has not been revived.

1961. Germany

Scottish curlers in 1931 played by invitation at Oberhof in Thuringerwald, mainly to enlarge the list of winter sports at the world championship games. No more came of it. In 1961, a German named Roussell, who had curled in Switzerland, organized a match at Garmisch in the Bavarian Alps. From this beginning, other matches were called elsewhere in successive years; clubs grew, and united in a German Curling Association, which has thirty affiliated clubs. International championships have since been held at Garmisch, where it all started, and German curlers number many hundreds.

1961. Holland

A few Dutch curlers formed the Amsterdam Curling Club in 1961. They played on the outside ice of a skating stadium, and travelled to Swiss and Scottish ice rinks for further practice. They still lack ice, for although they now have four hundred curlers playing at the Hague, Leiden, Rotterdam, Utrecht, Tilbury, and Assent, the best times are commanded by hockey players and skaters, and any ice time is most expensive.

1964. Belgium

Madame J. Francis, who had learned to play in Switzerland, founded a club at Liège in 1964. The game has since died.

1964. Denmark

With much help given by the Royal Club, a Copenhagen club was founded in 1964. It soon had fifty members and was running an international bonspiel for the Mermaid Cup. There has since been a steady growth in numbers and skill, with participation in European and world championships.

During the last decade, curling has continued to spread, sometimes to unexpected places. An *Ivory Coast* rink was opened at Abidjan in 1973. In *Wales,* curling began in 1974, when an indoor

137

rink was built near Liverpool at Deeside. There are now sixty curlers in six Welsh clubs. In *Finland,* curling began at Hyvinkaa in the late 1970s. It now has a hundred curlers, helped by Swedish coaches, and the game has spread to Helsinki. *Luxembourg* since 1976 has one club with forty members. They compete in the European championship. From *Japan,* there is report of a growing interest in curling, following its introduction in 1979 by Wally Ursuliak of Edmonton. Twelve years earlier, a demonstration of curling had been given at Tokyo by a United States curler, Dar Curtis. He had reported 'great enthusiasm' and thousands of onlookers, but no more came of it, at that time. It remains to be seen if the new introduction is more successful. Still more recently, curling has been introduced to *South Africa* by Erwin Sautter of Switzerland.

CHRONOLOGICAL TABLE OF CURLING BEYOND SCOTLAND
(An asterisk denotes that play has ceased)

1. 1760 Canada	9. 1880 Norway	17. 1964 Belgium*
2. 1775 England	10. 1890 China*	18. 1964 Denmark
3. 1832 USA	11. 1912 Italy	19. 1973 Ivory Coast
4. 1839 Ireland*	12. 1912 Austria	20. 1974 Wales
5. 1846 Sweden	13. 1920 France	21. 1976 Luxembourg
6. 1873 New Zealand	14. 1936 Australia*	22. 1978 Finland
7. 1873 Russia*	15. 1961 Germany	23. 1979 Japan
8. 1880 Switzerland	16. 1961 Holland	24. 1980 South Africa

The world wide dissemination of curling had important results for Scotland. Scottish rinks toured in nearly all the lands in which curling found lasting lodgement, and most of these lands sent rinks to Scotland. The world-wide exchange of ideas on techniques and rules, on crafts and tools, and on policies for play, has resulted in further evolution of the game throughout the world. The principal contribution to that continuing process has come from Canada. It seems not too much to say that this openness of curlers to evolutionary change saved the game from extinction at home, or to speak more positively, gave it lasting life.

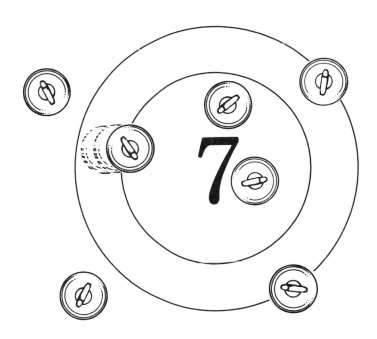

Curling Today: 1900-1981

A first short step into a new era was taken by Scottish curlers at the start of the twentieth century. They discovered the tarmac rink. John Macadam's road-metalling technique of 1816, which used whinstone chips packed close, had late in the century been found inadequate to meet the tearing action of motor car wheels. The answer was found in the 1880s (long after Macadam's death) by rolling in a top dressing of tar and chips. Twenty years later, curlers marked its practical application for rinks. Many clubs in the late nineteenth century had built artificial rinks and ponds on Cairnie's model, or else, if they were bigger or richer clubs, had laid concrete floors, which cost £100 a rink. Tarmac could be laid at one quarter of that price, and with far greater reward.

The first tarmac rink was laid in 1902 at Myreside in Edinburgh. Hundreds followed between then and the 1914 war; they revolutionized play. For example, in Dumfriesshire the Moffat club found that during the seven years ending 1913, a total of only forty days' play could be had on water-borne ice, while two hundred could be had on tarmac. In that same period and county, another record for one winter showed six days' play on concrete against seventy on tarmac; and that was simply because concrete (which developed humps and cracks) needed an inch of ice whereas tarmac could be sprayed at freezing point and the game played on a skin no thicker than a coin. Curlers declared such ice to be as good as that of Swiss rinks.

The tarmac rinks were lit at night by electricity or gas if near a town, or failing that by acetylene or paraffin lamps. Play was thus made available to far more people for a longer season than ever before in the past century, barring freak winters. With their appetite for the ice thus whetted, yet never satisfied by reason of short frosts, curlers were more than ready for the first of Scotland's indoor, artificial ice rinks – especially after digesting the reports of the first Canadian tour.

Indoor Ice

A private company in Glasgow, judging that skaters and curlers were present in sufficient number to yield profit, built the first

Edinburgh Ice Rink, Haymarket

Scottish ice rink at Crossmyloof in 1907. Its six rinks were open for play from October to May. Unlike Canadian rinks, which it otherwise resembled in having dining- and smoking-rooms, the Scottish rink (as in England) was iced with refrigerating machinery. Brine, chilled by compression of ammonia, was pumped by electric motor through pipes on the floor, thus freezing solid the water that covered them. When the rink was seen to be successful, three more were opened in 1912 – two at Edinburgh and one at Aberdeen. The first Edinburgh rink had a short life at Tollcross, but the second at Haymarket prospered, and remained open until 1978. The Aberdeen rink with eight sheets was Scotland's largest, until war closed it in 1917. Crossmyloof closed a year later.

In the new enthusiasm for indoor play, the Grand Match was staged five times at Glasgow and Edinburgh between 1908 and 1914. After the War, the experiment was not repeated. A national bonspiel on indoor ice was felt to be an unwelcome break with tradition, and with four hundred to six hundred rinks competing, not appropriate to the original purpose of bringing all together on one great day in the open. For all other purposes, the indoor rinks were seen now for what they were – the salvation of Scottish curling. The climate of opinion had changed so greatly, and hopes for the future had risen high, in part from the tarmac transition, and in large part from Canadian events. The reports of Canadian curling spread through the fraternity not only from the Scottish tour of 1903, but also from the Canadians' return visit of 1909, when they won the Strathcona Cup (presented by Lord Strathcona and Mount Royal, then president of the Royal Club).

Given access to good ice, Scottish curlers were appreciating as never before the skills of the twist, which could be seen by all free of the 'deep water' imperfections that tended to obscure the benefits. Sweeping skills could not help but improve, and granted peace younger curlers might now have paid some attention to the merits of pebbling the ice, which their elders still preferred to keep smooth (without experiment), or tried to conclude the disputes on hack versus crampit, and the best cut of sole for a curling stone – for on that age-old subject disagreement was kept alive by the difference between tarmac ice and indoor ice – but any such possible gains were suddenly aborted by war.

Curling took a long time, as did all other sports, to recover the ground lost by the huge drain in young manpower (Britain lost a million dead in action). A welcome aid to curling, after that disaster, came with an upsurge in the popularity of ice-hockey from 1927 onwards. The movement was accompanied by the building in 1928 of Europe's biggest ice-rink near the old site at Crossmyloof. Pebbled ice was at last introduced to the Scottish indoor curling rinks. In the 1930s, six more rinks were built at Ayr, Dundee, Dunfermline, Kirkcaldy, Murrayfield, and Perth. The second war then intervened. After it, ice-hockey had died but curling and skating recovered strength. Most of the rinks reopened, and such full use was made of them that a dozen more were added in the 1960s and 1970s. Now there are eighteen with room for more; curlers' numbers have kept pace with rink-growth.

In North America, the conversion to artificial ice was at first slower than in Scotland. Canada had less need. But the United States had been suffering mild winters, and in 1920 the first curling rink with artificial ice was installed at the Brookline Country Club in Massachusetts. A few others followed. The gains of consistent play were seen and artificial ice rinks began to multiply. Again the movement was halted by war. But the second war, unlike the first, was succeeded by a prosperity that in North America gave curling positive stimulation. Since the 1950s, most clubs have installed artificial ice plants.

The urgent need during two world wars to freeze food in bulk to withstand blockades, had brought new efficiency to refrigeration techniques – on both sides of the Atlantic. The plants in peace were adapted to give curlers better control of rink conditions. The vagaries of the seasons were a thing of the past; continuous play on consistent ice became gradually available to all who willed. And that in turn brought on the variety of developments that may be summarized as 'the modern game'.

The New Stones

Competitive curling, if it were ever to flourish, required the right kind of ice and the right stones. The rock as always had to be sound, hard, fine-grained, and 'elastic'; the need was for the finished stones to be made in matched pairs, uniform in overall dimensions, fashioned precisely at the cup-rims, and running equally on the ice. The man who gave this to the world's curlers was James Wyllie of

Mauchline in Ayrshire. After succeeding to the ownership of Andrew Kay's old factory at the Haugh, he moved in 1912 to a new site nearby, and there revived the best traditions of hand-craftsmanship. His grandson, James Wyllie, continues those rare skills of the mason today: Scotland has no other curling-stone maker. His family still trades under the name of Andrew Kay & Company.

During the first half of the century, granite for curling stones came from Ailsa Craig. The quarriers in the 1950s (named Girvan) found the accessible rock to be subject to spreading fracture; the waste grew huge in the 1960s. Each hundred tons felled from the cliff-face was yielding only a ton of sound blocks. To prise the pillars loose they used 'black powder', one of the least violent explosives, then split the pillars by drilling holes, into which wedges were hammered. The waste could not be reduced. Quarrying at Ailsa Craig was uneconomic. In the meantime, James Wyllie's two sons, Charles and Robert, had discovered a new source of equal-quality granite. They found it in 1946 on the sea-cliffs of Trevor in North Wales, on the coast of Caernarvon Bay. All rock for the world's curling stones now comes from there.

The rock arrives at Mauchline in 80-100 lb blocks, which have been roughly dressed at the quarry. Each block is passed through three machine-rooms, in none of which is the work automated. The shaping of the stone depends throughout on the judgment of the craftsman operating each machine. In the first room, it is chipped by heavy hammer to remove the worst protuberances, then screwed by side vices to the horizontal bar of a lathe. While it turns and chips fly, a circular steel cutter reduces it to approximately 50 lb weight, as judged by the mason's eye. A small hole is bored through the centre. It is still a rough block, if a more rounded one, when screwed to the lathe in the second room. A steel cutter, carefully adjusted from time to time by the mason, is brought to bear on the turning stone, again amidst flying chips. He brings it to within 2 lb of the weight and shape of a curling stone. When taken to room three, it is ground on a lathe with coarse carborundum to calliper measurements. The cup and rim are precisely positioned and shaped. The well-turned stone then goes to a double bench, which along either side has four wooden basins, each with a vertical shaft at centre-bottom. The stone is turned fast on one of these for polishing by hand. This is done first with a bar of fine carborundum, then

'Chipping'

'Turning'

144

'Honing'

'Beating'

145

'Polished and chiselled'

with a red sandstone, followed by a piece of water-hone, while a jet of water plays on the surface. The workman all this while concentrates on the stone's surface, eyeing it intently and judging it too by finger-tip feel, until he is satisfied that the stone is perfect. A final polish is given by a cloth pad clamped to the turning stone.

The stone comes off the bench as smooth and polished as marble.

146

The grain texture and colour-mottling are revealed in their full beauty. Some have a pink mottle (red Trevor), others a grey-blue (blue Trevor). The stones at this point are matched and go to a fourth room, where the striking bands are inscribed with a tungsten point, and then beaten out with a serrated hammer. Last of all, square countersunk holes are chiselled out top and bottom to take the handle-bolts.

The finished stone weighs 40 lb, plus $1^1/_2$ lb for handle and bolt. All cups are of 5″ diameter on both sides for indoor play. Nearly 90% of the product is for export to Canada. For the outdoor ice of Sweden and New Zealand, one side is given a dulled running edge of 4″ diameter, and the other a keen rim of 5″. For outdoor ice in Switzerland, where sun and shade contrasts are marked, the rims are $3^1/_2$″ dulled, and $4^1/_2$″ keen.

The introduction in bulk of matched sets to the Scottish ice rinks in the late 1950s was for their managers no small relief, apart from the benefit to curlers. Before that time, curlers owned and played their own stones, which had to be kept by their many hundreds in banked lockers within the rink-buildings. Staff were daily engaged in lifting them out to the ice in advance of each curling session, for they needed a few hours' cooling before play. Wyllie's product from Mauchline allowed the ice rink companies to stock their own stones and keep them on the rinks day-long, to the exclusion of stones privately owned. All gained. The curler's long-held ideal, a uniform stone of irreproachable quality, had been achieved. The fuller development of competitive play was under way.

Sponsorship

Canada in 1945 had 85,000 curlers. During the next twenty years, more than a thousand new rinks were built, accompanied by a seven-times increase in curlers' numbers to 600,000. The rise in numbers brought television to the scene, and more newspaper space. The mounting publicity attracted government grants for further building programmes. More people were given chance to play, more artificial ice rinks were opened, the clubs' curling programmes were diversified to provide for schoolboys and girls, women, and mixed play, in a most extensive variety of bonspiels. Many were sponsored by industrial firms. Curlers' numbers in Canada rose correspondingly to above 800,000 in the 1980s.

In this huge growth, sponsorship played a vital role. It came as a natural development from the previous century's presentation of prizes for competition, in which industries acted as patrons in exchange for advertisement. But more than trophies was needed. The great distances to be travelled in Canada for provincial or national competitions, with high transport and accommodation costs, stopped growth – unless these could be defrayed by a sponsor. The way this happened is illustrated by the first and foremost of Canada's sponsored competitions, the national championship, called the Brier.

In 1924, George Cameron of Winnipeg determined to bring together in closer friendship the curlers of east and west Canada. Their differences included Quebec's continuing use of irons. As a first step, he persuaded the Macdonald Brier Tobacco Company to give a trophy to Manitoba for annual competition, the winners to receive a goodwill tour to the eastern provinces with all expenses paid. Two years later, he and a group of curlers from Ontario convinced the Macdonald company of the need to replace the tour with a national competition. The company agreed and presented the Brier Tankard in 1927. The first Canadian national championship, henceforth called the Brier, was played off – using granite rocks – between the provinces at Toronto. After fifty years' sponsorship, Macdonald withdrew and their place was taken in 1980 by Labatt Breweries, but the Brier name was retained. It is the toughest and most prized of all Canadian trophies. Each team chosen to represent its province has to play more than a hundred games on its way to the finals – in local, district, regional, and then provincial playdowns. The winner of the Brier then represents Canada in the world championship (since 1959), and does so from a position of strength. Behind it are months of play and familiarity with big crowds and news coverage.

A source of much advantage to Canadian curling was the large-scale involvement of schoolboys. Boys' play had started around 1900, confined at first to the boys' own towns. Provincial competitions were long delayed by reason of expense. The Dominion Curling Association, which had been formed in 1935, and later became the ruling body under the name of the Canadian Curling Association, found a sponsor in Pepsi Cola. From 1958, the company met the expenses of a schoolboy curling championship, modelled on the Brier. It involved fifty thousand boys in provincial playdowns, leading to a national competition complete with banquet, trophies, and opening and closing ceremonies.

Within a year or two of that event, Dominion Stores Ltd sponsored a national championship for women, called the Dominion Diamond 'D' (later to become Macdonald's Lassie). Women's curling had begun around 1904. Their clubs grew into provincial and national organizations on the same pattern as the men's. That development brought in schoolgirls from the 1950s onwards, and soon afterwards popularized mixed curling. Sponsored competitions proliferated through the ice rinks. They so abounded, and the prizes became so numerous and rich on the provincial and national levels – they varied from motor cars to cash prizes of $10-25,000 – that the effect of such rewards on play had to be called in question. On the one hand, they encouraged skills and play among all classes of society, young and old, rich and poor, male and female; on the other, they encouraged from the 1960s commercial and professional attitudes to the sport, which many curlers felt to be not in the interests of the game – for example, when the Province of Ontario found employment for some of Saskatchewan's best curlers in hope of winning the Brier (which they did). The Dominion Curling Association in 1963 proposed banning such practices by reducing rewards, limiting play by men who earned money from curling, and controlling inter-province transfers. The proposals were voted down as being in themselves detrimental to the growth of play.

The controversy continues unabated. A possible if uncertain augury of things to come is the record of Paul Gowsell of Calgary. He won the World Junior Championship in 1976, in Scotland, and left school the following year aged 19. He turned professional: that is, without other source of income, his rink travelled the circuit of bonspiels in the western provinces. The biggest prize money there comes from three or four bonspiels like the Bessborough Classic at Saskatoon ($14,000), the Manitoba Open Cash Spiel ($25,000 of which the winner takes $10,000), and the 'World' open championship in Edmonton ($20,000), but there are many others, where the lesser sums to be won can mount up. In two years, Paul Gowsell was thus able to earn $125,000 – not counting other prizes, like the Vernon Car Spiel, or trophies like the World Junior, which he won a second time in 1978. His performance might seem likely to attract other young men to professional curling. Apart from the money, they can win titles and national fame. They may try but are unlikely

Paul Gowsell

to repeat his success. Gowsell's rink has been able to rise to third place in the Brier. It is difficult to keep a young rink together for any length of time, and Gowsell's original team has broken up.

Scotland with thirty thousand curlers and 620 clubs is not in this money league. The money depends on sponsorships, and on television coverage. The industries' attitudes to both have also been developing since the 1920s. Today, although much prize money is dispensed at the rinks by way of advertising, the bigger and more enlightened industries seek not only publicity for their products and services, but also fulfilment of social obligations. They sponsor, quietly, the arts and sciences, health and welfare, exploration and sport, and these in their many different aspects. Curling needs

150

money from sponsors, both on its social and competitive levels, and is worthy of having it; but no evidence has yet appeared, not even from Canada's Paul Gowsell, that prize money is required to needle a player into giving his best. A prize there must be, and one sufficiently valued. It need not necessarily have money value to induce tension. In the top competitive rinks, the player's love of the game then has all the spur it needs.

Competitive Curling and Tours

Canadian developments spread to the rest of the world through international curling tours and competitions.

It becomes important at this point to distinguish two levels of curling, social and competitive. Neither is superior to the other, they interpenetrate, they are equally valuable. Yet the one will sometimes modify the game more than the other. The great majority of curlers play for social reasons. They play to enjoy a friendly game, keenly contested, which can raise them to high excitement and long-lasting enthusiasm. A minority play at a competitive level, perhaps for title, or prize money, but also for the exhilaration of using the whole of themselves at a high pitch of nervous skill and tension. That high pitch can be struck only at keenly competitive levels, against equally skilled and experienced rinks, which have been winnowed out of their country's best. On either side the margin for error then becomes extremely small, nervous pressures build up, and the mind and will are stretched. Curling can become a way of life. Competitive curling is a main source of change in curling practice and techniques, and a mainspring of development from better ice to sponsoring.

The international tours were not in the above sense competitive, although matches were played. They were mainly social embassies, conducted to spread love of the game, to see how it was played in other lands, to make friendships, and to exchange ideas. Scottish teams visited North America in 1902, 1912, 1922, 1949 and 1955 (and in recent years). Canadian and United States teams toured Scotland in 1909, 1950, and 1952. These early tours had deep effects on the Scottish game. Some were quick, in so far as they hastened on better sweeping and attention to turning the handle; other effects were delayed, no more than preparing the way for change, for example to pebbled ice, the sunken hack, the slide delivery, and the take-out game as alternative to the draw game. In the long run they helped to move the conservative Scots to adopt Canadian innovations.

Following the first tour of 1902-3, the Royal Club had felt concerned about the slide delivery as then practised in Manitoba: it was not in accord with accepted rules. The second touring team of 1922 was therefore asked to sound out Canadian and United States opinion, and to report. The club might then act by a new ruling. The report read:

'There is no doubt that in many parts of Canada, and especially in Manitoba, players slide from the hack and retain hold of the stone for several feet before delivery, and the general opinion appeared to be that, although admittedly not strictly in accordance with the rule, this method of delivery was so universal that it would be impossible to get the majority of players to give it up. It was even hinted on one occasion by a leading Canadian curler that, should the Royal Club insist on the rule being strictly observed, it might easily prevent one of the principal Associations from being fully affiliated to the Royal Club. This would be extremely regrettable in view of the efforts made by the captain of the team during the tour to get all the Curling Associations in Canada and the U.S.A. to be fully affiliated to the Mother Club.'

The Royal Club agreed to allow slide delivery.

It was during the 1922 tour that the Scots introduced the long-handled push-brush to North America. Curlers there had exclusively used the short-handled corn broom, which they whipped back and forth on the stone's path; the Scots pushed the brush in short rapid strokes, never lifting it off the ice, and (if need were) applying ever more body weight as the stone slowed. There has been much discussion over the years on the two methods, and much controversy. Most Canadians prefer the corn broom, but the 'Scottish-style' brush is becoming popular on the grounds of lesser cost.

At home, until the 1960s, there was strong opposition to the slide delivery. The early ice rinks gave no encouragement to its introduction. The slide had been much aided by the American rubber-lined hack, sunk in the ice, and this the Scottish rinks did not at first provide – there was no time to ice-over the hacks between skating and curling sessions. They instead used the crampit before the

Canadian teams and the two sweeping styles. From (above) the 1980
and (below) the 1981 Air Canada Silver Broom World Championship.

wars; after which, a 'hack' that was no barrier to the slide. This was a modified tricker – a metal plate pronged on the underside and stuck down to the ice-surface. Many rinks use it today. But the Scots would not be converted to slide delivery before learning hard lessons at first hand in international competitive play, and not just through tours and reports. That opportunity was delayed until 1959, nearly forty years after the tour of 1922.

In the 1920s, the principal exponent of the slide delivery in Canada was Gordon Hudson. Watching him was a teenager named Ken Watson. Ken tried in vain to emulate his hero's slide to the outer ring – his ankle was not strong enough to support a slide on the side of the foot – until, practising once near midnight, he discovered by chance that if the rubber were removed from his left foot he could slide to the hog on the leather sole. He spent the rest of that winter perfecting his balance with nose down to the handle, so that he could sight through it to the broom. 'It was,' he said, 'just like sighting down a gun barrel. Believe me, it works.' Next year (1926), he won the Winnipeg bonspiel. Ten years later came the first of his three Brier wins. He emphasized, as a caution to other youngsters, that before achieving his spectacular slide to the hog, 'We had developed a true basic swing, so that the slide became only an exaggerated follow-through. Here is the mistake made by too many young curlers: they want to practise the slide first, so they never develop the swing along the line of direction. In the true gliding delivery, the stone is swung at the broom from the hack, and the slide simply follows the direction of the stone. The two are synchronized into a smooth-flowing, effortless motion.'

Ken Watson's fame and delivery-style had an electrifying effect on the Canadian young. It brought them on to the rinks in thousands – many committing the error against which he had warned them. The long slide is not in itself a recipe for success in curling. Some wanted to beat him at his own game, misconceiving what that was in their first wild enthusiasm. A comedy ensued at Montreal, when a schoolboy champion from Saskatoon, playing an exhibition game for his province, gave such powerful leg-thrust from the hack that he slid the entire length of the rink – and placed his stone on the tee *en passant*. The governing bodies of Scotland and Canada ruled that no slide might go beyond the nearer hog line (a rule recently amended to require only that the handle must be released before the nearer hog).

154

Tours and competitions in Canada brought home to the Scots the importance of training the young from their early teens. Not that boys' curling had been wholly neglected in Scotland. In the counties of Ayr and Dumfries especially, boys had been encouraged to play from the early nineteenth century. A few junior clubs were then founded, and tuition given in many of the parishes, as might be expected when their fathers were keen. But no strong growth spread across the country. Boys' curling almost vanished in the early twentieth century from lack of frost, the expense of indoor rinks, and the absence of leadership.

A first step to a new deal for the young was taken by Tom Murray of Biggar in 1929, when he gave the Murray Trophy for competition between curlers under 25 (now the trophy for the Scottish Junior Championship). Arthur Frame did more in the 1950s, when he started taking boys from two Glasgow schools to the Crossmyloof rink. Edinburgh schools soon followed his lead. Enthusiasm was instantaneous. Weekly school-league matches began in Glasgow and Edinburgh; a first inter-city match was held in 1961; more schools joined in the game, and the ice rinks co-operated. The movement spread, but more than this was needed. The young thrive best when self-responsible, and provision had still to be made for school-leavers. The initiative was first taken by Bill Horton of Glasgow, whose idea came from a stay in Canada. With the encouragement of his father and friends, and of the Scottish Ice Rink Company, he founded the Glasgow Young Curlers' Club, open to both sexes from their early teens up to 25. The movement spread through the land.

This promising growth of schools' and junior curling clubs came nearly twenty years after its Canadian counterpart, necessarily on a much smaller scale – sixty thousand boys were now engaged in Canadian competitions – but with no less keenness. The Royal Club in 1966 introduced a national schools' championship, and followed that with the Scottish Junior Championship open to curlers under the age of 21. Both are sponsored by the Bank of Scotland.

At home and abroad, notably in Switzerland, Scotswomen were curling in the early years of the century. They had formed an Edinburgh club in 1912 with forty members, otherwise numbers remained few until the ice rinks were built in the 1930s. Growth then began. Women joined existing clubs, formed sections therein, founded new clubs of their own, and in 1958 sent four rinks on a tour

Kandersteg, c. 1910

of Canada and the United States. In 1961, they established the Ladies' Branch of the Royal Club (now with over 220 constituent member-clubs). Married women, who can use the ice rinks in the mornings and afternoons, have thus far been the movement's mainstay. Among the many competitions for women, the principal are the Scottish Ladies' Championship, sponsored by the Clydesdale Bank, and the Junior Ladies' Championship, held for the first time in 1981 at Stirling. The winner of the former qualifies for entry to the Ladies' World Championship, which takes its place alongside the two other world championships, for men and juniors. In all three, the competing rinks are the national champions.

Switzerland, c. 1925

Perth, 1980. Ingvill Gitmark playing second for Norway in the
Royal Bank Ladies World Championship.

157

World Championships

Despite the great part played in development of the modern game by sponsorships, tours, competitions, and publicity, the strongest single influence on change in techniques, and on the twentieth century growth in numbers in Canada, Scotland, and other countries, has been the installation of artificial ice. The skilled making of indoor ice then allowed change in play, for the right stone was already there. Out of doors, the natural game was the draw game. On outdoor ice, curlers could not achieve the high degree of accurate shooting that made the take-out game practical tactics. Had it been otherwise, the take-out would have developed in Scotland before the draw game became set as traditional. This point was not at first appreciated in Scotland. Thus, despite the opportunity for change offered by the new ice-surfaces and pebbling, as displayed in Canada, and the good reports of them made by successive touring teams, the non-touring Scot was thrawn. He disliked the very thought of bare houses, and low scores, and wrongly conceived that no opportunity would be left for the real skills of the game, which to him meant drawing, and wicking, and creeping through a port. He failed to realize that the new Canadian play required these skills too.

The Scotch Cup

The event that changed the Scottish outlook was the inauguration of an unofficial world curling championship in 1959, and the annual exposure thereafter of Scottish curlers to the shooting of Canada's top rinks. In 1959, the Scotch Whisky Association offered the cup, a silver quaich, for competition between the champion rinks of Scotland and Canada. In Canada that meant the winners of the Brier; in Scotland, the winners of a national playdown, which in 1971 became the Scottish championship sponsored by Cutty Sark (and now by Lang's Supreme). The United States entered the competition in 1961. In succeeding years to 1967, they were joined by Sweden, Switzerland, Norway, France, and Germany.

In the first year, the Canadian challengers were a family rink from Saskatchewan, all four named Richardson, skipped by Ernie. It was they who brought to Scotland the long-slide delivery and the take-out game. Before they came, the Royal Club had agreed to their sliding to the hog and using the Canadian rubber hack, set deep, in place of the metal surface-hack used in Scotland. They won the cup with a splendid demonstration of all-round skills; not only that, they went on in subsequent years to win their own Brier four times, and the Scotch Cup four times (with only one change in their team, in 1963). Strong criticisms were made at first of their methods. Ernie Richardson was level-headed about his delivery technique and take-out strategy. He said again what Ken Watson had said before him: he insisted that the slide was essentially a proper follow-through to a good delivery, which must be mastered as thoroughly as the slide. He differed from Ken Watson in recommending that the swing and slide should be learned together, rather than the first before the second. 'The slide,' he added, 'should terminate as a natural part of the delivery, and no attempt should be made to lengthen the slide unduly.'

Ernie Richardson insisted on mastery of the draw shot, the need to maintain pressure on one's opponent, and to play varied shots according to the state of the game and the ice-pebbling. Hence, when he played the Scottish draw game at Perth he won that too. The Richardsons were indeed the world's best rink, fully versatile. After them, Canada continued to win – six years in a row, until the United States took the cup in 1965.

In the following year, the competing nations met at Vancouver, when they founded the International Curling Federation, which has since framed the rules for international competitions.

The Scots had been trying every means to break the Canadian grip of the world championship, until, at last, they realized the truth – the Canadian take-out game was superior in top-level competition, for which the *sine qua non* were great accuracy in shooting, fitness of body, and steel-like nerve. If Canada were to be defeated, it must be at their own game. The first Scots to act on the conclusion were four Perthshire farmers skipped by Chuck Hay. They gave themselves over to complete mastery of the Richardson technique and Canadian tactics. Ernie Richardson gave advice. In 1967 Chuck Hay's rink won the Scotch Cup at Perth.

That was a great day for the Scottish game, which took new life. It was also the last match for the Scotch Cup. The Whisky Association withdrew from sponsorship.

The Silver Broom

In 1968, Air Canada presented a new trophy, the Silver Broom.

Competition for it was officially recognized as the world championship. The eight competing nations were in 1973 joined by Italy and Denmark. It appeared at first that the Broom, like the Cup before it, had settled in Canada as immovably as the ancient *Hen* on its Lochmaben tee. Canada won five times in a row. This might seem inevitable, given Canada's curling population, which at this stage had risen to 750,000. But in every country the lessons taught by Canada had been learned. She lost the Broom in seven successive years, regaining it briefly only to lose once more. Why this should be has worried Canadian curlers. There can be no doubt that Canada keeps higher standards than Europe in competitive play, and that among far more curlers. It would seem that in the Broom a country's 'average standard' is quite over-ridden by some superior factor. Chuck Hay had shown that it is the dedication of the few top rinks (with the hard training of the teams' innate skills and their form of the day) that wins at highest competitive level. This was demonstrated eight times more in the Broom between 1973 and 1981, when Sweden and Switzerland each won it twice, the United States thrice, and Norway once.

Andrew McQuistin

THE WORLD CURLING CHAMPIONSHIP

THE SCOTCH CUP

Year	Site	Winning Skip	Country
1959	Perth	Ernie Richardson	Canada
1960	Perth	Ernie Richardson	Canada
1961	Perth	Hector Gervais	Canada
1962	Perth	Ernie Richardson	Canada
1963	Perth	Ernie Richardson	Canada
1964	Calgary	Lyall Dagg	Canada
1965	Perth	Bud Somerville	U.S.A.
1966	Vancouver	Ron Northcott	Canada
1967	Perth	Chuck Hay	Scotland

THE SILVER BROOM

1968	Pointe Claire	Ron Northcott	Canada
1969	Perth	Ron Northcott	Canada
1970	Utica, N.Y.	Don Duguid	Canada
1971	Megeve	Don Duguid	Canada
1972	Garmisch	Orest Meleschuk	Canada
1973	Regina	Kjell Oscarius	Sweden
1974	Berne	Bud Somerville	U.S.A.
1975	Perth	Otto Danieli	Switzerland
1976	Duluth	Bruce Roberts	U.S.A.
1977	Karlstad	Ragnar Kamp	Sweden
1978	Winnipeg	Bob Nichols	U.S.A.
1979	Berne	Kristian Soerum	Norway
1980	Moncton, N.B.	Rick Folk	Canada
1981	London, Ont.	Jurg Tanner	Switzerland

The world curling championship appears to be wide open. Scottish hopes have been given some encouragement after a long spell in the doldrums. In 1979, Jim Waddell's rink from Hamilton won the European Championship at Verese, in Italy, and Barton Henderson's Aberdeen rink won it again, somewhat precariously, at Copenhagen in 1980. Still better, two Stranraer rinks won the World Junior Championship in 1980 and 1981.

World Junior Championship

The idea of a world junior championship had germinated from a competition between Canada and the United States held at Toronto in 1970. Next year, they invited Scotland to enter a rink. Other countries of Europe joined in 1972 and 1973. At this point, Uniroyal Ltd assumed sponsorship. Scotland's entry each year is the winning rink of the Scottish Junior Championship.

The Royal Club had by 1975 seen the need to offer young curlers good training on their own rinks. In that year, they organised courses in coaching, at which selected curlers from the ice rinks were instructed by the national coach, Chuck Hay. The value of coaching and the success of the Young Curlers' Clubs as a breeding ground for high skills in the new generation, was made apparent when Andrew McQuistin's rink from Stranraer won the silver medal in the Uniroyal in 1979, and the gold in 1980. On that last occasion, at Kitchener, Ontario, his rink played the take-out game in spectacular manner. In the game against Switzerland, the Scots blanked nine ends; at the tenth and last, McQuistin had to play his last stone against a Swiss stone on the tee, half-guarded behind a Scots stone. He met that challenge to nerve with a perfectly judged double take-out, which left his own stone lying shot. Likewise, in the final against Canada, a report reads: 'Scottish fortunes were at a low ebb with Canada lying three, when Norman Brown transformed the game with a shot he will always remember – a brilliant triple take-out and lie, which raised the roof.'

The new generation of Scots has come a long way since their grandfathers toured Canada in 1922.

It seemed too improbable that Scottish juniors could win again in 1981, least of all a second time by another rink from Stranraer. Yet it happened, at Megeve in the French Alps. The skip was Peter Wilson. Surviving a shaky start to the competition, his rink defeated the United States in the semi-final and Canada in the final. Together with the world title, he won the award for the most sportsmanlike player on the ice – as McQuistin had too in 1979 and 1980. That the Uniroyal could be won twice running by two Scottish rinks against the huge reservoir of young North Americans, and Europeans too, bodes well.

The Stranraer teams were both coached by Chuck Hay. Both have expressed their indebtedness. The services of a national coach have become a vital element in the success of any young or inexperienced team. The stresses in a world competition are very high.

The Ladies' World Championship

The world-wide expansion of women's curling had been marked during the 1970s by the institution of national and international competitions, and finally by the Ladies' World Championship in 1979. This competition had first been conceived three years before at Duluth in Minnesota, during the Silver Broom. After gaining sponsorship from the Royal Bank of Scotland, and the approval of the International Curling Federation, it came to fruition in 1979, when eleven countries sent their champion teams to Perth to

Elizabeth Högström directs play in the final at Perth, 1981.

The rest of Elizabeth Högström's team in action on the same occasion.

compete for the Royal Bank trophy – Canada, Denmark, England, France, Germany, Italy, Norway, Scotland, Sweden, Switzerland, and the United States. The first three winners have been Switzerland, Canada, and Sweden.

The tough character of these world competitions is shown by the Swedish team's trial of endurance. Elizabeth Högström's Karlstad rink looked like winning the 1980 final against Canada, until, by a misjudgment in sweeping, their very last stone of an extra end ran an inch or so too far. In the fighting tradition of the game, they swore to come back. To do so, they had first to requalify in their own country as Sweden's best team for the 1981 European championship, which they won against Norway, and then again win the Swedish championship to qualify for the Ladies' World Championship at Perth. And there, by a brilliant display that gave the Canadian champions no chance, they won a 7 – 2 victory. Two other features of these games have been the youthfulness of the European teams engaged (relative to the Scots) and the benefit they seem to gain from the presence of coaches, which the Scotswomen lacked.

The Present

The Silver Broom, the Uniroyal Junior, and the Ladies' World Championship (which in 1982 moves from Perth to Geneva with a new sponsor), are the supreme tests in their own fields of all that a curler has learned and can give to the game. The scene at a world championship bears small likeness to a Scottish outdoor bonspiel as painted in my opening pages. The background hills, and wide skies, the low sun and blue shadows, the far-off mist, the bite of a wind off the moors, have gone. Most of today's young curlers have never curled out of doors, and have no wish to do so, or not at least for competitive purposes. Outside ice would not give them the game they want to play. Yet the indoor scene is most colourful in its own, very different way, and is most lively. The bright rink colours, the national flags and advertisements, the many colours of the competitors' dress, and the spectators banked in thousands above the ice-sheets, fill the stadium with the atmosphere of a great occasion. The players cannot help but respond to it. It keys them up nervously.

Before play begins, they may squat-jump to warm up, and to flex and relax muscles, or (without stones) make long delivery-slides; but once in play, consciousness of self goes; they are taken over by the natural excitement of the game and its mounting tensions of play closely competed. The wholeness of each man's concentration is seen in the very intentness of expression – his eyes fixed on the skip's broom, then upon stone and broom together after release of the handle – never changing while he slides through the rings. The player with his eye so close to the ice is in better position than the skip to direct the sweepers, and barks his orders. The sweepers push their brushes or flip brooms with a weight and rapidity and fast foot-movement exciting to watch for its cat-like precision. The overall rink-scene gives instant impression of athletic skill and supple movement. Even a casual glance shows this to be top quality

165

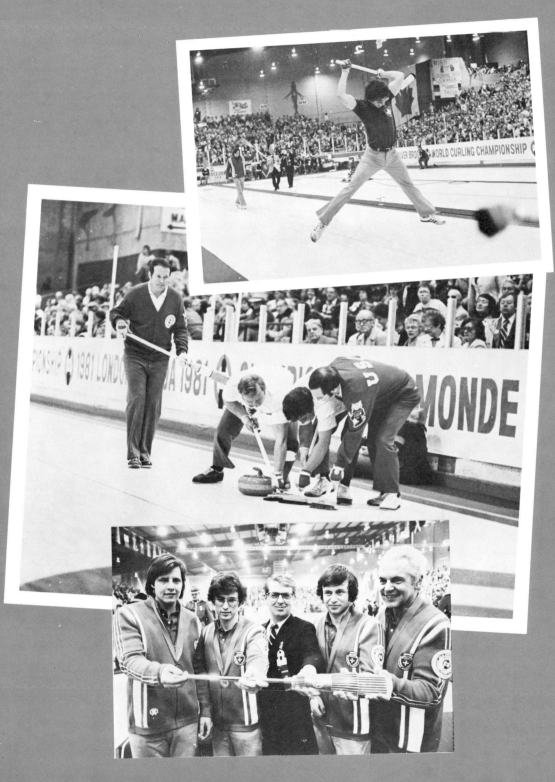

play. The main body of spectators are curlers themselves, or else know the game well enough to be involved; for that plainly shows, while they watch shots played, in the emotions that chase each other over their faces – surprise, incredulity, exasperation, downright disgust, and a joy to match the beatific vision.

Any rink that finds place in the Silver Broom must find it a heady experience, win or lose. When played in North America, whose people (like many others) are more demonstrative than the Scots, it ends with a razzmatazz of pipe bands, high-stepping girls, dancers, and processions – all in a too close imitation of a presidential election campaign to look natural for curlers, one would think, knowing the roots of the game. John Kerr might have a terse word for it, as he turns in his grave. Even so, he would rejoice in the world championship's great part in promoting curling through ten nations. The Scotch Cup of 1959 was like a chrysalis from which the Silver Broom has emerged as one of the principal events of world winter sports. No prize money is attached to the winning of it. The reward of honour may briefly come and quickly go among the nations; the chief and lasting glory of the Silver Broom has been its spread, amidst keen competition, of a strong international fellowship. The most important curling tradition of all has stayed the pace.

Curling has entered a new age. Knowing this, Scottish curlers have been acting on a sure instinct in keeping the Grand Matches alive, even through the lengthening years between one and another. The Royal Club still rules that the Grand Match will take precedence over all others. Each year it is organized in advance to the last detail. The summons rarely goes out, yet nearly a thousand rinks enter their names for it. From these, only six hundred can be chosen, for it takes two days to scrape the snow off three hundred rinks and then sweep and mark them. No longer delay can be risked. The last national bonspiel was called at the Lake of Menteith in February 1979, on eight inches of ice. The lake lies under the most southerly hills of the Trossachs. When the two thousand four hundred curlers stepped on to the ice, it was for many of the younger the first time they had played in the open air, or heard the boom of stones on a deep-water sounding board. The Menteith Hills rose close above; the woodlands fringed the ice; the sun shone out of a blue sky. The cannon fired and all happened just as described so often over the last hundred years and more.

The peculiar quality of the old game in Scotland, the one that

'. . . to forget all divisions of rank'. Raith Lake, Fife, c. 1860.

curlers most of all appreciated, had been its human bonding power. It brought players together on two levels. First, on the rink, where they keenly competed, trying for high standards of play. The game by its nature concentrated attention, brought close co-operation, and led men to forget all divisions of rank, thought, and person: that gave a sense of brotherhood on the rink, and a corresponding standard of behaviour. Second, off the rink, when they dined, drank, and relived the game. The convivialities followed naturally from a cold day in the open air with hard exercise; after which, the evening need of hungry men was for warmth, food, relaxation, laughter, and a shared enthusiasm for a great game.

In the modern, world-wide game, what has been lost, what gained, and what may survive?

The main loss in most countries had been the substitution of a game played within roofed walls for one played under the open sky.

The curler no longer plods home under a setting sun and the stars; his hunger is maybe less sharp, and his songs less spontaneous than they once were. In compensation, the gains from good ice, uniform stones, and nearly eight months' play each winter, have been immense, and need no recapitulation.

As to the game itself, *plus ça change, plus c'est la même chose.* It might seem to have changed almost beyond recognition, in its skills and competitive tensions. Yet I find it quite astonishing after reviewing four hundred years of curling, or three hundred years of its record, how little change has overtaken its essential, most valued elements. The rules of play have changed much in detail, but not in principal. The game has evolved from the crude to the refined in its tools and techniques, and its satisfactions to players, and more change is surely on the way. But the game is still as Thomas Pennant defined it in 1772: 'The object of the player is to lay his stone as near the mark as possible, to guard that of his partner, which had been well laid before, or to strike off that of his antagonist.' The more essential element to survive is the social fellowship. Last century the spirit of brotherhood was emphasized more heavily than now, yet was not foisted on the game by some deliberate, ethical policy; it was innate in the character of curling itself; it emerged naturally; each and every member had to give close attention to his fellow's play, and back it up by himself giving his best. Everyone had to co-operate. A man's walk of life ceased to count. His play was all that mattered. The game was unifying. And so it is today, because the curlers of all nations have agreed to keep it so.

The Rink and Rules of the Game

As amended at the Annual Meeting of the Royal Caledonian Curling Club, 1980.

Section A – The Rink

1. The length of the playing area shall be 42.06 m. (46 yards). It is recommended that the width of the playing area shall be a minimum of 4.75 m. (5.20 yards) and that, where possible, the ice be continued a further 1.22 m. (4 feet) or more behind each Foot Line.

2. The length of the Rink from the Foot Line to the Tee shall, subject to the provisions of Rules 5 (Section A) and 1 and 2 (Section H) be 38.40 m. (42 yards).

3. The Tees shall be 34.75 m. (38 yards) apart and – with the Tees as centres – Circles having radii of 1.22 m. (4 feet) and 1.83 m. (6 feet) shall be drawn.

4. Additional inner Circles may also be drawn. Dividing lines may also be drawn or barriers placed between adjoining Rinks.

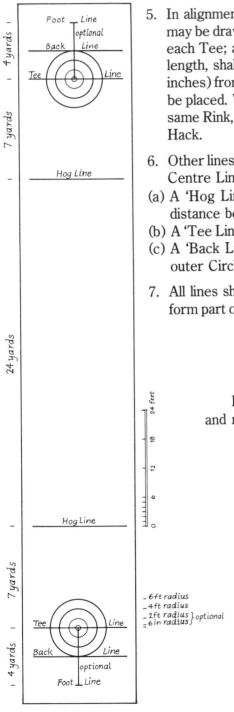

5. In alignment with the Tees, lines, to be called Centre Lines, may be drawn from the Tees to points 3.66 m. (4 yards) behind each Tee; at these points Foot Lines 45.72 cm. (18 inches) in length, shall be drawn at right angles, on which, at 7.62 cms. (3 inches) from the Centre Line, the inside edge of the Hack shall be placed. When Hack and Crampit are both being used on the same Rink, the Crampit shall be placed immediately behind the Hack.

6. Other lines shall be drawn across the Rink at right angles to the Centre Lines as in the diagram, viz:–

(a) A 'Hog Line', distant from each Tee, one-sixth part of the distance between the 'Foot Line' and the farther Tee.

(b) A 'Tee Line', across each outer circle and through each Tee.

(c) A 'Back Line', behind and just touching the outside of each outer Circle.

7. All lines shall be as in the accompanying diagram, which shall form part of these Rules subject to Rules 1 and 2 (Section H).

Diagram to be drawn on the Ice
and referred to throughout the Rules as

THE RINK.

174

Section B – The Curling Stone

Shape, Weight and Dimension of Stone

1. (a) Curling Stones shall be of a circular shape,
(b) No stone, including handle and bolt, shall be of greater weight than 19.96 kgs. (44 lb), or of greater circumference than 91.44 cms. (36 inches), or of less height than 11.43 cms. (4.5 inches).

Substitution, Reversing and Breaking of Stone

2. (a) No Stone shall be substituted for another (except under Rules 2c (Section B) or 5 (Section C) after a game has started.
(b) During a game, the sole of a Stone may be reversed, provided the player be ready to play when his turn comes.
(c) Should a Stone be broken, the largest fragment shall be counted for that End, the player using another Stone, or another pair, thereafter.

Stone Rolling Over, Handle Quitting

3. (a) Any Stone which rolls over in its course, or comes to rest on its side or top, shall be removed from play immediately.
(b) Should the handle quit the Stone in delivery, the player is entitled to replay the shot.

Section C – Delivery of Stone

1. Left-handed players shall play from the Hack or Crampit placed on the right-hand side of the Centre Line, and right-handed players shall play from the Hack or Crampit placed on the left-hand side of the Centre Line.

Delivery from Wrong Hack or Crampit

2. (a) A Stone delivered from the wrong Hack or Crampit should, if possible, be stopped in its progress and removed from the ice.
(b) However, if the Stone so played has come to rest or struck another Stone, the played Stone shall be removed from play and the displaced Stone or Stones be placed as nearly as possible where they originally were, to the satisfaction of the

opposing Skip; both Skips should agree upon the position, but, failing agreement, the Umpire shall decide.

Release of Stone

3. (a) In the delivery of the Stone, the Stone shall be released from the hand before the Stone reaches the nearer Hog Line.
(b) If the player fails to so release the Stone, it shall be removed from play immediately by the playing Rink. If the Stone has struck another Stone, the played Stone shall be removed from play by the playing Rink and any displaced Stone shall be placed as nearly as possible where it originally lay to the satisfaction of the opposing Skip.

Holding Stone, Returning for Another Delivery

4. No player may hold his Stone and return to the Hack or Crampit for another delivery if the Stone has reached the nearer Tee Line, in which event the Stone shall be removed from play by the playing side.

Playing Wrong Stone

5. Should a player play a wrong Stone, a Stone belonging to his Rink shall be put in its place.

Playing out of Turn

6. (a) If a player should play out of turn in his Rink, the Stone so played should, if possible, be stopped in its progress and returned to the player.
(b) Should the mistake not be discovered until the Stone has come to rest or has struck another Stone, the End shall be continued, as if it had been played properly from the beginning, but the missed Stone shall be played by the player missing his turn as the last Stone for his side for that End.
(c) Where the Skips agree that a Stone has been missed but are unable to agree as to which player missed his turn, the lead of the Rink which made the mistake shall play the last Stone for his rink at that End.
(d) Where two Stones of a Rink are delivered in succession at the same End, the opposite Skip shall remove the Stone played by mistake, replace to his satisfaction any Stone displaced by the Stone played by mistake and continue the End as if the mistake had not occurred, and the player who delivered the

Stone played by mistake shall redeliver it as the last Stone for his rink at that End.

(e) Where a player delivers three Stones at one End, the End shall be continued as if the mistake had not occurred and the fourth player of his rink shall deliver one Stone only at that End.

Section D – The Game

1. All games shall be:
(a) of a certain number of Ends; or
(b) by time
as may be agreed on, or as fixed by the Umpire at the outset (see Section I).

Composition of Rink, Order of Play, Disqualification, Accident

2. (a) Every Rink of players shall be composed of four-a-side, each player using two Stones, and playing each Stone alternately with his opponent.

(b) Any Rink not having its full complement of four players shall be disqualified except in the case of illness or accident during the game, in which case the first and second players shall play three Stones each.

(c) When, in a competition, owing to illness, accident or any other valid reason, a player is unable to play in any round, he may be replaced by another player as substitute, provided this substitute has not already taken part in that competition in any other Rink. A substitute may play in any position in any round but not higher than the position of the curler he is replacing. The Skip shall declare any substitute in the first round of a competition or the Rink in the first round will be understood to be the entered Rink. No Rink shall take into play more than two substitutes in any game, match or competition. All substitutes must be eligible in terms of the rules of the competition.

(d) The Rinks opposing each other shall settle by lot which side shall lead at the first End, after which the winners of the preceding End shall lead, and shall continue to do so if any extra Ends be played.

(e) The rotation of play observed during the first End of a game shall not be changed.

(f) The Royal Club may modify the above rules to meet with requirements of a specific competition.

Finishing of Games Played by Time

3. (a) When a game is being played by time, no End shall be started after the finishing time signal has been given, except where extra Ends are required.

   (b) If the time signal has not been given when the last Stone of the last played End has come to rest, then another End shall be played. (*Note:* the intention of this rule is that another End will not be started if, when the time signal is given, the last Stone or any Stone in play is still in motion.)

Stone not Clearing Hog Line

4. A Stone which does not clear the farther Hog Line shall be a Hog and shall be removed from play immediately except where it has struck another Stone lying in play.

Stone Crossing Back Line

5. A Stone having crossed the Back Line, and lying clear of it, shall be removed from play immediately.

Stone Touching Sides of Rink

6. Any Stone which in its progress touches swept snow on either side of the Rink, or raised sides and divisions of Indoor Rinks, shall be removed from play. But, if a Stone crosses a dividing line drawn on the ice between Rinks or sheets and returns to finish within the Rink clear of the dividing line, it remains in play, provided it has not touched any object in the adjoining Rink. (See 10b).

Running Stone Touched

7. (a) If, in sweeping or otherwise, a running Stone be touched by any of the side to which it belongs, or by their equipment, it shall be removed from play, but if by any of the opposing side it shall be placed where the Skip of the side to which it belongs shall direct, in a position as nearly as possible where he estimates it would have come to rest.

   (b) Should the position of any Stone be altered by such affected Stone, the Skip opposed to the side at fault shall have the right to replace it in a position as nearly as possible where he estimates it rested before its position was altered.

178

Displaced Stones

8. (a) If a Stone which would have affected the course of a running Stone is displaced by the playing rink, the running Stone shall be removed from play and any affected Stone shall be placed as nearly as possible where the opposing Skip considers it originally lay.

(b) If a Stone which would have affected the course of a running Stone is displaced by the opposing Rink, the Skip of the playing Rink shall replace any affected Stone as nearly as possible where he considers it originally lay or would have come to rest.

(c) If displaced in a way other than stated in (a) and (b) of this rule, both Skips should agree on the positions to which the Stones are to be returned.

Measuring of Shots

9. (a) Skips may call for shots to be measured, but not before the last Stone of the End being played has come to rest.

(b) Measurements shall be taken from the Tee to the nearest part of the Stone.

Scoring

10. (a) Games shall be decided by a majority of shots. A Rink shall score one shot for every Stone which is nearer the Tee than any Stone of the opposing Rink.

(b) Every Stone which is not clearly outside the Outer Circle shall be eligible to count, even if touching a dividing line.

(c) In the event of the score being equal, play may be continued for one or more Ends, as may be agreed on, or as provided for by the conditions of the Game or Match, or as may be fixed by the Umpire.

(d) An End is decided when the Skips (or acting Skips) in charge of the House at the time agree upon the score for that End.

Section E – The Skip: His Authority, Privileges, and Responsibilities

1. (a) The Skip has the exclusive direction of the game for his Rink.

(b) Subject to Rule 2 (e) Section D, he may play in any position in the game he pleases.

(c) When his turn to play comes, he shall select one of his players as acting Skip.

(d) He may, however, return to the House for brief consultation.

(e) The Skip of the playing side has the choice of place, and he shall not be obstructed by the other Skip.

(f) Only Skips (or acting Skips) are entitled to stand within or behind the circle.

Section F – The Players: Their Duties and Responsibilities

1. (a) Players, during the course of each End, shall be arranged along the sides, but well off the centre of the Rink.

   (b) No player, except when sweeping according to rule, shall go upon the centre of the Rink.

   (c) No player shall cross the Rink when:
       (A) a player is about to play; or
       (B) in front of a Stone which is in motion.

   (d) No player, other than the Skips and acting Skips, shall stand within or behind the Circle while play is proceeding.

   (e) Each player shall be ready to play immediately when his turn comes.

   (f) A player shall not take more than a reasonable time to play.

   (g) No player shall use footwear or equipment which may damage the surface of the ice.

Section G – Sweeping

1. The sweeping shall be under the direction of the Skips.

Method of Sweeping

2. The sweeping shall be across the course of the Stone and no sweepings shall be left in front of a running Stone.

Limitations of Sweeping

3. (a) The player's side may sweep the ice from Tee Line to Tee Line but any Stone set in motion by a played Stone may only be swept by the side to which it belongs, except behind the Tee Line, where both Skips have an equal right to sweep.

(b) Only Skips (or acting Skips) shall be allowed to sweep behind the Tee Line and shall not start to sweep an opposing Stone until the Stone reaches this line.

Section H – Abnormal Conditions

Shortening or Changing Rink

1. (a) If from any change of weather after a game has begun, or from any other reasonable cause, one side should desire to shorten the Rink, or to change to another, and if the two Skips cannot agree, the Umpire shall, after seeing one End played, determine whether and by how much the Rink shall be shortened, or whether it shall be changed, and his decision shall be final.

(b) In no case, however, shall the Rink be shortened to less than 29.26 m. (32 yards) from the Foot Line to the Tee.

(c) Should there be no Umpire, or should he be otherwise engaged, the two Skips may call in any neutral curler to decide, and his powers shall be equal with those of an Umpire.

Stopping, Postponing a Game

2. (a) Should the Skips not agree, the Umpire shall, in the event of the ice appearing to him to be dangerous, stop the game.

(b) He shall postpone the game, even if begun, when the state of the ice is, in his opinion, not fitted for testing the curling skill of the players.

(c) Except in very special circumstances, of which the Umpire shall be judge, the game or match shall not proceed, or be continued:

(i) when a thaw has fairly set in;

(ii) when snow is falling and likely to continue during the game or match; or

(iii) if darkness comes on to prevent the played Stones being well seen by players at the other end of the Rink.

(d) In every case of such postponement to another day the game or match, when renewed, must be begun anew.

Cleaning Rink

3. (a) At the completion of any End, either of the Skips may call upon all the players to clean and sweep the entire Rink.
(b) If objected to, this shall be subject to the approval of the Umpire.

Sweeping

4. When snow is falling or drifting, both Skips have equal right to clean and sweep the ice behind the Tee Line, except while a player is being directed by his Skip.

Section I – The Umpire

1. An Umpire may be appointed in any game, match, or competition. He shall be a member of the Royal Club and shall be acquainted with these Rules.

2. The duties and powers of an Umpire shall be the general superintendence of a game, match, or competition, the power of settling disputed shots, enforcing these Rules and other questions that may arise in course of play.

3. He shall satisfy himself that all the players are duly qualified.

4. He may depute a neutral curler who is a member of the Royal Club and acquainted with the Rules to act in his stead.

5. His decision in respect of all questions affecting the game, match, or competition shall be final.

Glossary

Words no longer in use are marked with an asterisk.

Arridge, or **arris:** the rim of the concavity on the stone's bottom.

Back-ring weight: a stone thrown just hard enough to reach the back of the house.

*****Baugh:** rough or soft ice, not keen (now called 'dour' or 'drug').

Besom: a curling broom.

*****Biassed ice:** ice not level.

Blank an end: to strike stones out of the circles so that no one scores, or to choose not to score with the last stone played, thus to retain the advantage of playing the last stone in the next end – see Rule 2(d), Section D.

*****Board:** the rink.

*****Boardhead:** the area enclosed by the large circle round the tee (now the 'house').

Bonspiel: curling match in which many rinks are engaged.

Borrow: the amount of left- or right-hand draw taken by a stone; **borrowing:** aiming to one side of the tee, sometimes by several feet, in order to reach the mark (where ice is not true).

Break an egg: touch a stone lightly.

*Broughs: the circles round the tee (now the 'house').

Bunker: uneven ice, usually water-borne.

Burn: to touch a moving stone played by one's own side.

Bury: to place a stone behind a guard so that it cannot be directly hit.

Button: the tee.

Chap and lie: to strike an opponent's stone and drive it out of the house, while one's own stone lies within.

Chip: to hit another stone lightly on its side.

*Cock: the tee.

*Core: a rink of players.

Crampit, or ***crampbit:** spiked metal foot-plate. (*Early type,* strapped to the foot; *since mid-nineteenth century,* an iron sheet fixed at the foot-line).

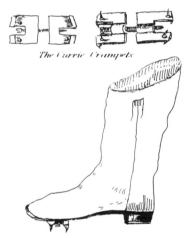

The Curie Crampets

Cup: concavity on the sole of a curling stone.

Curl: curling movement of a stone caused by turning the handle.

Dolly: wooden skittle marking the tee.

Double: a shot that strikes two stones off the circles – 'a double take-out'.

Dour ice: ice not keen (same as 'baugh').

Draw: (1) to play gently to a spot within the circles;
(2) the curl taken by a stone.

Draw weight: the momentum given to a stone just sufficient to bring it into the circles.

Drive: to strike.

Drug ice: soft, damp, or slow ice.

End: the period of play in which both teams deliver all their stones in one direction (the score is then reckoned and play begins again from the opposite end).

Fall: a slope on the ice causing the stone to move in a direction opposite to that expected from the rotation of the handle.
Also called a run-back.

Fill the port: block the space between two stones.

Freeze: a stone that comes to rest close in front of another, touching it or nearly so.

Front end: the lead and second players in a curling team.

Front ring: the part of the house nearest to the hog.

Give ice: estimate by the skip of the curl needed for the next shot, given by placing his broom at the point to which the curler should aim if his stone is to curl into the right position.

*Gleg ice: keen ice.

Guard: a stone that covers another.

Hack: the foothold from which the player delivers: formerly just a hollow notch cut in the ice, now a metal or wooden plate, surfaced with rubber, screwed into the ice, or a rubber cup sunk into the ice.

Hack weight: a take-out played with sufficient weight to reach the hack.

Head: the build-up of stones in the house during play.

Heavy: a stone thrown with too much force.

Hog: a stone that stops short of the hog-line.

House: the area within the outer circle round the tee.

*Howe: the middle of the rink, coursed by thrown stones.

In-handle, or **in-turn:** turn of the handle to rotate stone clockwise.

*In-ringing: gaining good position by rebound from the inside edge of another stone. (Now called 'in-wicking'.)

In-wick: a stone that glances off the inside edge of another to gain a good position.

*Kowe, or **cowe:** a broom.

Kuting: old term for curling.

Kuting stone: oldest form of stone, without a handle.

Lead: a rink's first player.

Lie shot: to place a stone nearest to the tee.

Light: a stone thrown with too little force.

Loofie: the oldest form of stone (from Scots *loof,* palm of the hand).

Lose handle: a stone that loses its initial curling motion.

*Mar: to interfere with a running stone (same as 'burn').

Narrow: a stone delivered inside the line of the skip's brush.

Out-handle, or **out-turn:** turn of the handle to rotate stone anti-clockwise.

Out-wick: to strike a stone on its outer edge to drive it nearer the tee.

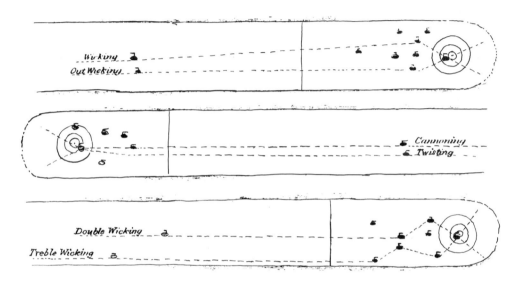

Pat-lid, or **pot-lid:** a stone lying on the tee.

Pebble: blistered ice-surface, made by spraying water.

Pick up: dirt or broom-hairs that interfere with a stone's path.

Points Game: a singles game to test accuracy in selected shots. (One or two stones are set up in the house or close to it, prior to play, and shots are then played to test drawing, wicking, raising, chipping, guarding, etc.)

Port: narrow opening between two stones.

Quacking: causing stone to rock from side to side on its run up the rink.

Raise: to promote stone towards the tee by bump from in front.

*Rebut: to deliver with force.

*Red(d) the rink: to strike out opponents' stones.

Rink: (1) playing space; (2) the four members of a team.

Roll: movement of a stone after hitting a stationary stone off-centre.

Rub: a light glance off the edge of another stone.

Shot: the stone that is nearest the tee during the play of an end. It may refer too to the playing of a stone, e.g. a narrow shot – one played inside the broom; or a wide shot – one played outside the broom; or a firm shot – one played fast.

Skip: the director of a team. (Formerly also called a brandey, master, oversman, hin-haun, leader, or douper.)

Soop: to sweep.

*Souter: to win without allowing opponents to score.

Spiel: a curling match. Same as bonspiel.

*Spend a stone: waste a shot by intentional wide delivery.

Swingy ice: ice on which a stone has more than normal draw.

Take-out: a stone given enough momentum to strike another stone out of play.

Tee: the mark or bull's-eye at the centre of the house. Also named button, and in the past cock, cockee, gog, gogsee, toe-see, tozee, and wittyr.

Tramp, tricker, trigger: an early form of the modern hack – a spiked iron plate from which the stone was delivered, fixed at the foot-score.

Wick: a stone that gently strikes the edge of another stone to glance off at an angle.

Wide: a stone delivered outside the line of the skip's brush.

Bibliography

1632 Kilian, C. (Cornelis Van Kiel), *Etymologicon Teutonicae Linguae.* Utrecht edn. *See also* revised Amsterdam edn. of 1642.

1638 Adamson, H., *The Muses Threnodie.*

1774 Pennant, T., *A Tour in Scotland: 1772.*

1811 Ramsay, J., *Account of the Game of Curling.*

1830 Broun, Sir Richard, *Memorabilia Curliana Mabenensia.*

1833 Cairnie, J., *Essay on Curling and Artificial Ice Making.*

1840 Bicket, J., *Canadian Curler's Manual.*

1874 Brown, J., *History of Sanquhar Curling Society.*

1884 Taylor, J., *Curling. The Ancient Scottish Game.*

1890 Kerr, J., *History of Curling.*

1904 Aflab, F.G., *The Sports of the World.*

1904 Kerr, J., *Curling in Canada and the United States* (a Record of the Tour 1902-03).

1908 Syers, E. & M., *The Book of Winter Sports.*

1914 Grant, J.G., *The Complete Curler.*

1924 Marshall, M.H., *The Scottish Curlers in Canada & the U.S.A.* (a Record of their Tour in 1922-23).

1929 Mobbs, A.N. & McDermott, F., *Curling in Switzerland.*

1950 Creelman, W.A., *Curling, Past and Present.*

1950 Watson, Ken, *Ken Watson on Curling.*

188

1960 Weyman, H.E., *An Analysis of the Art of Curling*
(1942 edn revised).

1963 Richardson, E., & others, *Curling.*

1968 Howe, R.A., *The Development of Curling in the United States*
(Ph.D. thesis, Indiana University).

1969 Lindsay, P.L., *A History of Sport in Canada 1807-67*
(Ph.D. thesis, University of Alberta).

1969 Welsh, R., *Beginner's Guide to Curling.*

1970 Gerszi, T., *Bruegel and His Age.*

1973 Grossman, F., *Pieter Bruegel.*

1976 Durkan, J., *Paisley Abbey in the Sixteenth Century:*
The Innes Review, Autumn, p.112.

1980 Maxwell, D. & others, *The First Fifty* (a record of the Brier).

1980-81 Royal Caledonian Curling Club, *Annual.*

1980-81 Royal Caledonian Curling Club, *Constitution & Rules.*

Magazines and Newspapers:

1838 *North British Advertiser,* 26 May and 23 June.

1853 *Scotsman,* 16 Feb. Report on Grand Match.

1873 *Daily Review,* 13 Feb. Report on Grand Match.

1914 *Country Life,* 3 Jan. *Ancient Curling,* by Bertram Smith.

1977 *Scotsman,* 28 Dec. *Historic Tournament on Ice,* by David B. Smith.

Canadian Curling News
Canadian Curling Review
Curling World
North American Curling News
⎫
⎬ Articles and Reports, 1967-81
⎭

Index